Competency-Based Education and Behavioral Objectives

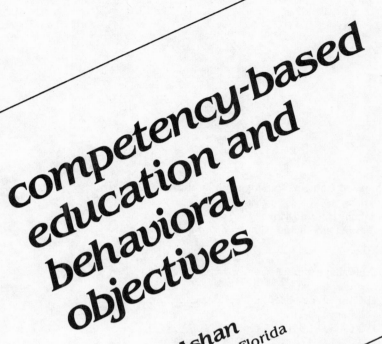

competency-based education and behavioral objectives

H. H. McAshan
University of North Florida

EDUCATIONAL TECHNOLOGY PUBLICATIONS
ENGLEWOOD CLIFFS, NEW JERSEY 07632

Library of Congress Cataloging in Publication Data

McAshan, Hildreth Hoke.
    Competency-based education and behavioral objec-
tives.

    Bibliography: p.
    Includes index.
    1. Competency-based education. 2. Behaviorism
(Psychology) I. Title.
LC1031.M32   370'.732   78-31160
ISBN 0-87778-132-X

Printed in the United States of America.

Library of Congress Catalog Card Number:
78-31160.

International Standard Book Number:
0-87778-132-X.

First Printing: April, 1979.

Preface

This volume is intended to assist in meeting the needs of a variety of educators, such as: (1) those professional educators involved in teacher training; (2) those administering educational programs; (3) those teaching in K-12, junior college, and university classroom situations; and (4) students who are training to assume educational roles in the future. In addition, people assigned teaching responsibilities in any field, such as nursing, insurance, and government sponsored training programs, may find this book equally helpful.

The specific intent of this work is to provide a functional description of Competency-Based Education (CBE) and to identify the advantages of such programs, as well as to identify current problems which tend to reduce the effectiveness of CBE. In addition, this book deals with the techniques for writing and operationalizing appropriate types of competencies (goals) and performance objectives, so that many of the problems identified within the text may be either reduced or eliminated.

The writing of behavioral objectives and the CBE programs subsequently developed from the use of objectives represent drastic program changes and considerable innovation when compared with traditional programs. Many of the past program change movements have been illusionary in failing to serve the profession, and none have managed to transform the profession into one which accomplishes all of its major goals. Sponsors of the CBE and behavioral objective movements will need to understand and overcome many already existing problems if these movements are going to make stronger contributions to education than did previous ones.

To place the CBE and behavioral objective movements into proper perspective, one should recognize that they must take their places alongside previous innovations, such as team teaching, homogeneous grouping, lengthening the school day, modular scheduling, differentiated staffing, the new media, and a host of others. The behavioral objective and CBE movements are subject to the same enthusiasm, political motivation, economic frustrations, and other attributes as were all the other movements. None of these previous movements were able to transform the total instruction or the profession in any significant manner. Each did contribute something to the learning situation, but the most significant gains were mostly situation-specific.

Currently, contributions of CBE based upon the use of behavioral objectives fit this same mold. In other words, the benefits, if any, of CBE are situation-specific. This means that the merits of individual CBE programs are confined to the situation in which they are developed; that strong generalizations cannot be made from them; and that, in most instances, they are not likely to be diffused into new situations involving different faculties and students.

Change is a phenomenon of all ages. Yet, there are strong forces that keep educational systems from changing and which pose a threat to all innovation. These forces include: (1) barriers in the community at large, (2) political barriers, (3) economic barriers, and (4) most importantly, barriers within the educational community itself. Each of these barriers, if not overcome, can be fatal to educational innovation. The first three barriers involve problems of: (a) the threat imposed to the public of changing from the "status quo"; (b) the fear of additional cost for materials, facilities, and staff; (c) the recognition that educational systems in our society are in deep financial trouble; and (d) the red tape involved both politically and economically in promoting change through the local, state, and federal bureaucratic structures. These are all significant.

It is, however, the fourth group of change barriers, the barriers within the educational community, which are, perhaps, the most destructive for the advancement and diffusion of worthwhile CBE programs. First, there is the *weak information base* upon which behavioral objectives have been formulated and CBE programs have been founded. Little solid research and experimentation has been accomplished in this area. Most CBE programs have been developed as "piecemeal" improvements over the experience-based programs which were the traditional practice of teacher education institutions.

In addition, many educators and psychologists have become unwitting disseminators of educational propaganda that is actually destructive to curriculum development. The specific propaganda being exploited includes:

(1) the false premises and theoretical bases upon which much of the use of behavioral objectives and subsequent CBE programs have been based;

(2) the misuse of goal statements by defining all goals as broad or abstract statements of intent;

(3) the implication that competencies and behavioral outcomes are the same thing;

(4) the use of behavioral outcomes as ends rather than as evaluation indicators to be used in determining successful competency achievement;

(5) the statements which indicate that goals are less specific than behavioral outcomes;

(6) the establishment of tasks rather than content as the focus of education; and

(7)   the use of student performances as the primary basis for determining teacher accountability.

Despite the fact that many outstanding educational leaders, theorists, and practitioners have become aware of these and related problems, very little in-service education has been offered, or even sought, by the faculty members involved, as a means for identifying and remedying the knowledge base problems.

Second, there are few, if any, *institutional change agent positions* in most universities, junior colleges, and public school systems. This means that there is no person with both the knowledge and academic or political clout to influence the program decisions that are made. As a result, most CBE program components represent, primarily, the thinking "off the top of the head" of the committee appointed to decide the nature and extent to which CBE will be developed and implemented in each separate institution.

Despite the two barriers within the educational community that have been named—weak information base and lack of institutional change agents—and others not dealt with in this Preface, the behavioral objective and CBE movements do appear to have more to offer than many previous curricular changes, because there appears to be something in them for everyone. Persons interested in goal-setting or competency identification, analysis and development of teaching strategies, and program evaluations of all types can find ample opportunity to pursue their interests in this movement. Administrators concerned with program accountability can produce better and more overtly observable data than they were able to produce under the traditional experience-based approach. Researchers can find new opportunities to utilize their expertise. Students become more aware of what they are expected to learn and how their success will be determined, and it becomes easier to communicate instructional program contents to their parents.

Regardless of all of these and other attributes of behavioral objectives and CBE, there are many dangers involved in writing appropriately stated goals and objectives and in converting them into viable educational programs. Until these problems are overcome, perhaps it is fitting and best that all CBE programs should remain situation-specific. It is toward assisting the educational community to do a better job with their existing programs in the face of the steadily increasing number of problems being identified that the author has exerted his efforts.

This text may be viewed as having been developed in five parts. First, Chapter I focuses upon the false premises and knowledge base problems, which have resulted in many educators' concluding that the use of behavioral objectives is ruining, rather than benefiting, instructional programs.

Second, Chapters II, III, IV, and V are designed to introduce the reader to Competency-Based Education and the need for CBE. Chapters III, IV, and V give in-depth coverage to the three essential components of CBE; (1) competencies, (2) behavioral outcomes, and (3) the instructional delivery system.

Third, Chapters VI, VII, and VIII are designed to instruct the reader in how to write meaningful behavioral objectives. The technique is developed in Chapters VI and VII, whereas, cognitive objectives are operationalized by use of the cognitive taxonomy in Chapter VIII.

Fourth, Chapters IX and X are designed to train the reader to develop behavioral objectives according to the taxonomies of the psychomotor and affective domains.

Finally, Chapter XI offers the reader instruction in developing non-learning oriented performance objectives for use in establishing employee accountability for work responsibilities assumed in programs employing the management-by-objectives or systems analysis processes. The Appendix provides a Sample Course Module.

H.H.M.

Table of Contents

xi

Competency-Based Education and Behavioral Objectives

I.

Mythical Illusions
Concerning Curriculum

"We ought not to be over-anxious to encourage innovation, in cases of doubtful improvement, for an old system must ever have two advantages over a new one; it is established and it is understood."

—Cotton

"We think so because other people all think so; or because—or because—after all, we do think so; or because we were told so, and think we must think so."

—Lidgwick

"People act not according to the truth but according to what they think to be the truth. Control what people think and you will control the way that they act."

—Marx

CHAPTER GOALS

The reader should:

1. acquire comprehension of six myths which have greatly reduced the effectiveness of the behavioral objective and competency-based education movements;

2. develop comprehension of major premises that have been established by the rigid behaviorists which create untenable problems that may eventually destroy the behavioral objective-CBE movements.

Why do the average educational practitioners think whatever they think or believe whatever they believe about any innovative practice? Is it because they have carefully researched each issue and found the pending change to be irrefutably an improvement? Could it be that the will of an otherwise intelligent professional is overcome by powerful individuals or vested-interest groups within the profession?

Neither of these two answers can fully explain the fast growth and wide acceptance accorded the behaviorist movement with regard to the writing and use of behavioral objectives. This writer would estimate that the current emphasis on behavioral objectives received its impetus in the early nineteen sixties and that the growth of the behavioral movement was dictated by the educational media available at the time. This media consisted primarily of a programmed text authored by Mager[1] and some supporting filmstrips by Popham.[2]

In essence, these materials constituted just about all of the known items available for training educators in behavioral objective writing during the early years of the movement. Gradually, other materials began to appear, but, by-and-large, they were mostly reflections of the Mager-Popham materials and strongly repetitious in both the viewpoints presented and in the definitions used to define behavioral objectives.

Early interest in behavioral objectives by the greater educational community was centered upon the uses of behavioral outcome statements to insure the validity of content selection for curriculum and to improve teacher evaluation practices. This point was well taken, since behavioral outcomes fit well within accepted evaluation practices. Traditionally, this included: (1) identifying the correct type of evaluation performance; (2) identifying appropriate situations in which to observe measurable performances; (3) determining proper success level standards; (4) deciding upon how to collect the desired data without contaminating the results; and (5) analyzing the data and reporting the outcomes to the appropriate decision-maker.

Tyler[3] outlined the processes of educational evaluation as including: (1) identification of general objectives (goals); (2) specification of these goals in behavioral terms; (3) specification of situations in which the behavior could be observed; (4) devising and applying instruments for making observations; and (5) relating evidence obtained to the original objective.

Instructional evaluation practices were, at least indirectly, improved by the use of behavioral outcomes. This change was not due so much to a change in the methods and techniques of evaluation, but, rather, to its enhancement through teachers' and other educators' concern with measurement and evaluation practices. In addition, the concept of criterion-referenced measurement began replacing the concept of normed measurement in many classroom situations. From this early beginning, the CBE movement has gradually emerged.

The behavioral objective-CBE movement has been spurred on by the increasing demands for (1) accountability, (2) instruction which allows students to proceed at their own rate, and (3) increased general program quality that is relevant to the goals of society.

Most educators will agree that the use of behavioral objectives enables teachers to place a stronger focus on instruction that is tailored to meet specific goals with success being determined by evidence obtained through specific behavioral outcome performances. Yet, there is obviously a lack of agreement about what should constitute a behavioral objective in the first place.

Present Status of Behavioral Objectives

One can predict that both the behavioral objective movement and the resulting programs of competency-based education will fail to reach their potential value if some of the current problems in writing and using behavioral objectives are not eliminated or modified. Currently, "what is the case" is more frequently than not far removed from "what ought to be the case."

Unless there is a concerted effort by institutions of higher education and educators in general to come to some feasible agreement on what behavioral objectives should be and the functions they serve, the real promise of their development and use is unlikely to be realized. The implementation of CBE programs to date has been, primarily, a function of the individual program developer's understandings of the definition of the behavioral objectives which he/she has accepted. These understandings, which are situation-specific, are likely to result in some very serious problems that will affect overall instructional program development as the behavioral objective and CBE movements continue to grow.

The conceptual framework within which one views a behavioral objective and the assumptions one must make according to the conceptual approach one chooses to accept are crucial. These two choices will not only determine how objectives will be written, but will also determine how competencies are stated and evaluated. Whether enabling strategies will be selected to achieve the competencies or to achieve evaluation performances, and what will ultimately be considered to be the ends and means of any resulting CBE program will be decided as well.

Obviously, if one school system develops curricula in which competencies are considered to be ends and behavioral outcomes are used as evaluation indicators, and another school system bases its curricula upon the idea that behavioral outcomes are both the ends of instruction and the evaluation indicators, then the curriculums developed in one system or the other are getting *raped* or, at least, *seduced*.

Herzberg[4] has an effective way of stating this case. He indicates that rape "can be considered an unfortunate involuntary occurrence" whereas seduction "may be worse" since seduction is a situation "in which the victim volunteers to become a party to his own downfall." It is unfortunate that, under the guise of innovation and change, educators can be seduced so easily.

The writer believes that the rape or seduction of the curriculum that has taken place is the direct result of several myths which have shaped the behavioral objective movement and which have been allowed to remain virtually unchallenged. By myths we refer to the historical events that have occurred which were based on fallacious reasoning and have served to explain the current illfounded beliefs held by the rigid behaviorists. The list that follows represents a few of the more significant myths to which we refer:

(1) Goals should be defined as broad or abstract intents.

(2) Goals are best defined by behavioral outcomes; thus, competencies should be stated as behavioral goals.

(3) Behavioral outcomes should not be primarily considered as a means for evaluating competency achievement.

(4) Specifically stated behavioral outcomes, rather than goals, are the ends of instruction.

(5) Goals are less specific than behavioral outcomes, thus, using goals as ends results in abstract or trivial objectives.

(6) Teacher accountability should, primarily, be based upon the behavior or performance of their students.

The remaining pages of this chapter will be devoted to the analysis of these myths and to an explanation of the fallacies they represent.

Myth Number One: Goals should be defined as broad
                              or abstract intents.

Mager[5] defines a goal as "a statement describing a broad or abstract intent, state, or condition." Since his book, *Preparing Instructional Objectives,* represents, by far, the most widely read resource used for learning to write behavioral objectives, it is only natural that other users of the "outcomes approach" for writing behavioral objectives have treated goals or competencies as being broad, general, or global statements of purpose or intent.

There is, however, little basis to define goals in these terms, other than the fact that *some* goals can fit into this category. What about all of the rest of the goals which can be as specific as an educator desires to make them? Defining goals as broad or abstract has not always been the case, and such a categorization should not be allowed to remain unchallenged.

Smith[6] has questioned the logic or rationale of the outcomes approach type of behavioral objective. He particularly questions the logic of defining goals as broad, general, global, or abstract purposes or intentions. He writes, "In the first place, when goals (purposes, intentions) are stated in very general or vague terms, precise evaluation is impossible. Perhaps an even more important consideration is that when goals are vague, teachers and students are unable to exercise intelligent and effective choices concerning the means for attaining the goals." He concludes the paragraph with, "Stating a behavioral objective is, then, primarily an attempt to increase teaching and learning effectiveness through clarity and mutual understanding concerning goals." This final statement places goals, rather than behavioral outcomes, as the desired instructional ends.

Good[7] provides three useful definitions for a goal. They are: (1) "an object toward which an organism strives with conscious or unconscious purpose that guides activities toward a specified end"; (2) "the aspiration of a student in terms of academic achievements"; and (3) "an object capable of satisfying a need and toward which motivated behavior is directed." The Webster[8] dictionary defines a goal as "the end toward which effort is directed."

Neither of these two authoritative resources refers to a goal as being broad or abstract. Both do agree, however, that a goal represents a purpose or an end. In addition, they seem to agree that goals are what student efforts in achievement should be focused upon. Goals have always been thought of in this vein and should still be defined within this context.

One must assume that the Mager definition was intended to represent an operational definition to set the stage for other concepts he was developing in his pioneering efforts to operationalize behavioral outcomes. Even so, defining terms operationally does not warrant the definition of a term to mean whatever you want it to mean or to change its basic meaning. In fact, operational definitions are intended to clarify a word's use and to prevent it from being too abstract or misleading.

Mager[9] refers to goals as being "fuzzies" and describes his steps for writing goal statements as abstract intents from which behavioral outcomes will be developed. He stated, "use whatever words are comfortable, regardless of how fuzzy or vague they may be. This is the place for such words." He then advocates using whatever words are comfortable regardless of how vague they are. His contention is that it doesn't matter how broad the words are, since their purpose is only to create a starting point that is "politically useful" to serve as a purpose for the later statement of behavioral outcomes, which he defines as "specific objectives."

To refer to either goals or competencies in this manner prohibits educators from seeking to identify them with the amount of specificity that is required, if they are to serve the real purposes of instruction. Goals in all reality can be broad global statements or very specific statements. The more specificity with which each goal or competency is stated, the better success in achieving it can be measured and the more specifically enabling strategies can be developed to achieve each intent.

Examples of the differences between a broad and specific cognitive goal stated for the same instructional content area are as follows:

(1) Graduate students should acquire the understandings necessary to develop and use performance objectives effectively in carrying out their instructional responsibilities.

(2) EDA 611 students should acquire knowledge of specific terms which are important in the development of skill in writing behavioral objectives.

The competency identified by the first goal, stated at a broad or high level of abstraction, is not very suitable for behavioral objective development because it has lost most of the necessary specificity from the learning intent. In other words, understanding can mean memorization, comprehension, application, analysis, synthesis, or evaluation. Thus, success in achieving this competency or goal statement cannot be measured with any degree of authority, since many behavioral outcomes might be acceptable as its evaluation indicators. In addition, the accountable learner group, the term performance objectives, and the content are not well defined. Of course, if the person writing the competency does not know what target he/she is shooting for, or is not interested in communicating it clearly to the learner, he/she may very well be willing to accept any behavioral outcome or group of outcomes as being satisfactory. This, however, would be an example of poor planning and would lead to poor evaluation practices.

The second example goal statement is very specific. It identifies the specific learner group that will be accountable for achieving the competency. The learning task has been specifically defined to mean level one of the cognitive taxonomy, the acquisition of knowledge through memorization, and the content has been limited to that which relates to terms relating to skill in writing behavioral objectives.

The broadness or abstractness of a goal is always relative. In other words, there are times you may desire to identify a global area and you will choose a rather abstract goal to represent your specific intent. At other times, you will wish to identify a goal which represents a very narrow bit of content and, in this case, you will state it very specifically.

The specificity of the goal or competency statements in an instructional module will be determined by the person or persons performing the systematic analysis of the unit of content to be presented. The realities of the teaching situation, as well as the content area, are taken into consideration. If a course is to represent a 16-week semester assignment, its objectives may be stated less broadly than would be the case in the event that the identical content were to be presented on a ten week basis. Another factor may be whether or not the competency represents a field-based situation or, merely, the development of classroom level knowledge and comprehension. It is within this context that we suggest that competencies must always be somewhat situation-specific.

Myth Number Two: Goals are best defined by behavioral outcomes; thus, competencies should be stated as behavioral goals.

Approximately ten years after his very successful book on writing instructional objectives, Mager[10] wrote another text in which he apparently attempted to clarify some of his concepts relating to behavioral outcomes. In this text, entitled *Goal Analysis*, he proposes to define goals as behavioral outcomes. He states, "Goal analysis is a procedure useful in helping you describe the meaning of the goals you hope to achieve." On another page, he says, "The function of goal analysis is to define the indefinable, to tangibilitate the intangible ... to help us say what we mean by our important but abstract goal." ... "to identify the main performances that go to make up the meaning of the goal." Perhaps, if he had not unnecessarily defined goals as being broad, abstract intents, this book would not have been necessary.

The type of goal analysis to which this book refers is not a true goal analysis, but an analysis of behavioral outcomes. Due to his personal magnetism, writing expertise, and the creative humor which depicts goals as "fuzzies," the book's readers are mostly unaware that they have been skillfully led away from the content, the substance from which curricula are developed. Content is immediately replaced by behavioral outcomes or performance tasks.

Geis[11] called it correctly when he wrote, "Traditionally, the world of education is a world of content. Something vaguely called knowledge is at the core of all that the educator does. And the analyses that are made tend to be in terms of content analysis —rather than in task analysis ... when the educator thinks of what he/she is going to teach, he/she does not think of a performance or task but rather of a subject matter."

Mager's[12] goal analysis really becomes task analysis, which he defines as "a careful description of what the competent person does or is supposed to do when he is doing a job." The fact that performing work on a job is a response made possible by what a person has learned, but not the learning intent itself, appears to make no difference to a rigid behaviorist.

In a true goal analysis, assuming one has actually begun with an abstractly stated goal or "fuzzy," a person would, eventually, end up, after one or more levels of analysis, with sub-goals, each stated to identify a much narrower area of content than that identified in the original abstract goal. For example, let us look at Figure 1.1, which represents a goal analysis performed by a home economics instructor in one of Florida's state junior colleges.

Figure 1.1 reveals that the content area of Basic Textiles can be broken down over several levels of abstraction until the broad area is, finally, represented by the specific competencies a teacher chooses to state as instructional goals. This process can be referred to as a goal setting process and involves a true goal analysis in which broad areas of content can be reduced to many narrower components or sub-goals.

Figure 1.1. Sample goal analysis.

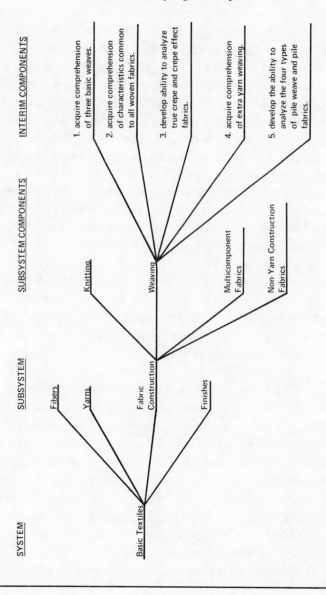

This content breakdown by a systematic analysis procedure reveals that there is considerable difference between a goal analysis of content and a task analysis to determine outcome performances. In addition, it is easy to see why goals have been relegated to such a subordinate position by the behaviorists. It is only by destroying the concept of the goal as being a content oriented end that the behavioral outcomes can assume the role of ends.

Obviously, behavioral outcomes do not define goals. Used as they are represented in the text, *Goal Analysis*, they, actually, prevent the careful definition of broad goals that would occur through a true goal analysis, resulting in the identification of the narrower sub-goals of which each broad goal is composed. Content is replaced by performance which are unlike entities. Division of competencies should result in more specific sub-competencies, and division of behavioral outcomes results in more specific outcome performances, but neither one will ever result in the other, when used in the proper context.

We all know, however, that competencies go well with behavioral outcomes, when the competencies are correctly used to represent instructional ends or intents and behavioral outcomes are used as assessment modes or evaluation indicators to determine success in competency achievement.

Myth Number Three: Behavioral outcomes should not be
primarily considered as a means for
evaluating competency achievement.

The general literature of the behavioral objective and competency-based education movements is heavy with references depicting the connection between writing behavioral objectives and program evaluation. Dressel[13] stated, "the desire to determine (measure) the extent of growth, development, or change had led some educators to insist that objectives should be presented in behavioral form." According to this concept, he believes a primary purpose for stating educational objectives in such specific terms is so "that the performance of the individual can be observed and evaluated." He further elaborated that the word " 'evaluatable' may in some respects be equated with 'behavioral.' "

Anderson[14] helped establish the relationship between the objectives of an instructional program and the program's evaluation when he wrote, "without well-stated objectives there is no basis for making any judgment as to whether or not the program has achieved the desired goals." Piper[15] stated, "writing objectives, then, involves the skills of identifying what is to be learned and when it has been learned." In his article, assessing learning is equated with determining when learning has occurred.

McAshan[16,17] defined evaluation as referring to the performances, activities, behavior, or instrumentation that is used to demonstrate the level of success obtained as an outcome of the activities undertaken to achieve a goal. Harrow,[18] author of *A Taxonomy of the Psychomotor Domain*, supports this definition and the use of behavioral outcomes primarily as evaluation indicators. In chapter four of her taxonomy, all example behavioral objectives are stated with the behavioral outcomes used as evaluation components only.

Simons[19] criticized the concept that the goals of instruction can best be conceived in behavioral terms. He made the point that knowledge and behavior are not synonymous and said, "no doubt the emphasis upon specific behaviors simplifies measurement, but this simplification calls into question the validity of the measurement itself. In short, it is not known what, beyond behavior, is being measured."

Smith,[20] in making a case for the importance of clarity and mutual understanding concerning goals, wrote that "precise evaluation is impossible" if goals are vaguely stated. Armstrong[21] *et al.* pointed out the relationship of goals being evaluation indicators for goal achievement by stating "the trick is to supplement each announcement of purpose with a stated behavior to be observed and (to know) how to measure that behavior." In addition, they cautioned that "some type of behavior that is observable will have to stand for or represent the intellectual performance we have intended."

Thomas[22] made the point that observable actions, measurable behaviors, and performances are not his intents, but are what he calls "behavioral evidences." ..."observable behaviors are simply partial evidence that the instructional objective was attained. ...there are numerous behaviors that provide evidence of understanding ... what has been termed behavioral objectives are really limited samples of evidence, behavioral evidence that instructional objectives have been attained."

Even Mager[23] inadvertently admitted that behavioral outcomes are evaluation indicators when he gave his procedures for performing a goal analysis. He stated, "Jot down the performances that, if observed, would cause you to agree the goal has been achieved." This can only mean that the behavioral outcomes are the measures of success used to determine competency (goal) achievement.

The literature quoted and many additional references that are available clearly substantiate the fact that behavioral outcomes should be primarily used for purposes of evaluation. Perhaps the greatest fault with the strict behaviorists is not that they don't recognize behavioral outcomes as measures of evaluation, but that they play the point down in order to promote these outcome behaviors as performance goals with the status of ends.

Myth Number Four: Specifically stated behavioral outcomes, rather than goals, are the ends of instruction.

In chapters four, five, six, and nine of the text, *Goal Analysis*, Mager[24] attempts to establish behavioral performances rather than goals as the true ends of instruction. At one point, he stated, "we are not terribly concerned with whether the performance that defines a goal is really the meaning of the goal." Later, he commented that in determining the behavioral outcomes by goal analysis, you are sometimes led "to a definition of the goal you started with, and sometimes it leads to the definition of another." Compounding this premise further, he states, "Ask yourself this question: Is it reasonable or practical to achieve this goal? If the answer is no, reverse the goal to one that is reasonable or practical to achieve."

Throughout his book, he implies that it is only the behavioral outcome that has real value. In chapter five, he specifically refers to the outcome behaviors as being the desired ends by stating, "you may occasionally find some items that describe procedures rather than outcomes, means rather than ends." He maintains this viewpoint, as do other behaviorists, despite the fact he is fully aware that this type of specific objective is without visible purpose. In chapter four, he states it this way: "Just about any time you show someone your specific objectives, write the goal they define on the same page. It is often difficult for a layman to understand the significance of an objective; if he sees only the specifics, he is likely to grunt, 'Why would anybody teach anybody that?' If he sees the goal on the top of the page, he is less likely to emit such disturbing sounds."

This writer thoroughly agrees with that comment. No specific objective defined only as a behavioral outcome and criterion makes sense or has any purpose other than that of an assessment mode. It cannot stand on its own value, but must be seen in relationship to a true goal or competency before it can become worthwhile for instructional purposes.

None of the writers using the "outcomes approach" behavioral objective writing technique appear to recognize the significant differences that exist between a learning outcome (designed to specify the desired cognitive, affective, or psychomotor capabilities a learner should develop as part of his repertoire of skills, abilities, and feelings) and a behavioral outcome that should be used as an assessment indicator to establish that learning has taken place. These differences will be cited later in this text by references to the works of authors, such as Gagne, Simons, and Gronlund, as they define learning outcomes as (1) capabilities that remain part of the learner, (2) knowledge rather than behavior, and (3) understanding rather than behavioral outcomes. The premise that desired behavioral outcomes and learning outcomes or purposes are the same thing is unacceptable to this writer, to others quoted, and to many other educators. Again, we state that learning outcomes are ends, and behavioral outcomes are means to determining success.

Shane and Shane[25] recorded some interesting and pertinent comments during a personal interview with Ralph Tyler, the person considered to be the earliest pioneer or father of the present-day behavioral objective movement. The interview included questions such as what he meant when he referred to behavioral objectives and how he viewed the way they were being used today. The following quotes were given by Tyler in answering these questions:

> "What I mean by behavioral objectives is a statement of what teachers are trying to help students learn from their instruction. ..."
>
> "I think many people who are trying to use behavioral objectives today perceive them as very specific kinds of behavior. If they consider that is what schools are all about, they are confusing knowing answers with being educated. ..."

Perhaps Tyler's most profound statement was the one given as his summary comment to the interview. He stated, "Behavioral objectives are of value only insofar as carefully phrased ones serve as tools in helping instruction attain its real goals." It is clear that Tyler, as is the case with an increasing number of other professional educators, views the goals rather than the assessment behavior as the ends of instruction.

The competencies are the most important part of a CBE program. They represent the instructional ends to be achieved by the learner. If the competencies are not appropriately chosen, it won't make any difference how good the enabling activities are or how well success is evaluated. The program will not be a good one. Thus, it is imperative that performance outcomes retain their role as assessment techniques and not be chosen as program ends.

Myth Number Five: Goals are less specific than behavioral outcomes, thus, using goals as ends results in abstract or trivial objectives.

Goals are not less specific than behavioral outcomes. They just happen to represent a different component of a CBE program. Goals can be viewed as being less specific if they are rated according to standards that are established for program evaluation. However, since they are not intended to serve as evaluation components, there is no reason to judge them by assessment criteria.

Perhaps the fuzziest fuzzies of them all are the behavioral outcome statements. A behavioral outcome represents an evaluation component that in and of itself consists of a performance and a criterion without a stated purpose. A behavioral outcome must be associated with the competency which it represents in order for it to have any real value.

Again, at the risk of being redundant, we will quote for the second time a phrase that illustrates the point from one of the Mager[26] texts. "Just about any time you show someone your specific objectives, write the goal they define on the same page. It is often difficult to a layman to understand the significance of an objective; if he sees only the specifics, he is likely to grunt, 'why would anybody teach anybody that?' " This appears to be a direct admission that an objective's purpose is not really indicated in the behavioral outcomes and that it is the *goal statement* that must be referred to, in order to establish purpose.

Competencies, hence goals, are intended to communicate information, such as who is the learner or learner group and what is the learning task with reference to content and domain. Insofar as they communicate these factors adequately, they can be said to be specific. Behavioral outcomes should communicate evaluation data, and they are judged to be specific according to whether or not assessment performances and criteria are correctly specified. Neither the goal nor the behavioral outcome must meet criteria that do not represent its own function.

Goals are not given the status of behavioral objectives until behavioral outcomes are included under the "Goals Approach" behavioral objective writing technique. Behavioral outcomes are sponsored by the behaviorist movement as being behavioral objectives, although they represent objectives without a purpose. Thus, one must conclude that the question of objective triviality must refer only to the "outcomes approach" statement of behavioral objectives.

The major question posed in an article written by Deming[27] was whether or not behavioral outcomes were necessarily trivial. He stated, "One major criticism of the performance approach to instruction is that it tends to promote the teaching and learning of trivia." He offers the texts and curriculum guides prepared in many school systems as evidence of such trivia.

He further stated that "the ability to state learning outcomes in performance terms cannot, in and of itself, serve to structure the content of instruction. ... To evolve beyond trivia, the practice of translating goals into performance terms must be built, at the very least, upon both increased sophistication in the technical skills of formulating performance objectives and increased mastery of one's discipline or area."

Thomas[28] made the point very clearly when he wrote, "Failure to distinguish between objectives and evidence of their attainment has led to the vexing problem of triviality. Waks[29] was very specific when he said, "it would seem likely that instruction according to (the behavioral) model may promote trivial goals despite their ready detection." On the same page, he indicated that the possibility exists that in some areas only trivial goals can ever be made to conform to the requirements of the behavioral approach.

It is the "outcomes approach" objectives stated without specific goals or content purpose that are suffering from the numerous claims of triviality. Educators who first identify specific competencies within their behavioral objective statements are not subject to such complaints.

Myth Number Six:: Teacher accountability should, primarily, be based upon the behavior or performance of their students.

Waks[30] published an article in which he examined the validity of arguments against behavioral goals. In his discussion, he stated Popham's scheme for teacher evaluation as being "Teachers will be judged by reference to their ability to produce results rather than on the many bases now used as indices of teacher competence." He further indicated that Popham says, "teachers should be judged on this basis alone." . . . "Bases for teacher evaluation other than the ability to produce desirable changes in behavior are nothing but 'folklore' and 'mysticism.'"

To this writer, the concept of basing teacher accountability upon student performance is utterly preposterous. No one can assume the major role in being responsible for student learning other than the student himself/herself. Teachers can be held accountable for the processes involved in teaching, but there is no way they can "learn" *for* the student.

Referring back to the parent process of the behavioral objective movement, Management By Objectives (MBO), we find that goals are established and employees are assigned the responsibility of achieving these goals. Each employee is accountable for achieving those goals to which he/she has been assigned and for which he/she has accepted responsibility. Only the employee who has direct responsibility for achieving a goal and whose on-the-job performance can be the determining factor in whether or not the goal is achieved is held primarily accountable.

In the case of instructional objectives, goals and objectives are set which are assigned to students and for which students must accept responsibility. Only the student with direct responsibility for learning can be the determining factor in achieving the goals for which he/she is accountable. All other factors, including the instructional efforts of the teacher, must be considered as trivial in relationship to the factor of students assuming the responsibility for achieving their own goals and objectives. Only the student can determine his/her own amount of preparation, only the student can take the test or display the necessary adjustment to his/her social environment.

The major point is that *accountability should be limited to evaluation of factors which the accountable person can produce by his/her own decisions and actions*. A teacher can lead a student to the trough, but only the student can make the decision and effort to drink the water it contains.

Deming[31] says, "The focus of accountability must be on the process rather than the product of instruction. Process accountability holds the teacher responsible for knowing his subject matter, knowing his students, and using professionally sound instructional procedures." He views the issue of whether teachers will or will not be evaluated according to "product accountability," sometimes referred to as "consequence accountability," as a major consideration to be made in program planning. He supports his contentions by summarizing Jencks' study, which indicated that school related factors account for only a fraction of the differences found in student achievement.

According to the MBO process, goal setting should begin at the top of an organization, not in the middle or at the bottom. Carried to the zenith of accountability, responsibility for student performance can be traced to the state legislatures and their politically motivated decisions, which do not place education into the forefront of their appropriate commitments. Usually, education receives whatever is left over after most other state obligations have been financed. Accountability can then be traced through the state departments of education, the local school boards, the district level administrators, and the local school administrators. Also accountable are the parents and peers of each student and other contextual factors which make a difference in a student's life.

The point is that it would be unfair to evaluate any of these groups based upon how well students perform, because none of them can produce positive results based upon their own decisions and actions. All are just small cogs in a large wheel. So is a teacher, despite the fact that he/she is visibly exposed to the students.

Niedermeyer and Sullivan[32] spoke directly to this point when they referred to instructional accountability as being a joint responsibility of boards, district level administrators, and teachers, not just the teachers alone. They said, "Serious injustice, however, is rendered by the increasingly popular practice of assessing pupil performance on the objectives and holding teachers accountable for specific performance levels." They further stated, "professional responsibility for instructional success should not be placed solely upon teachers." ... "Teachers should not accept the notion of instructional accountability, if it is treated as their exclusive responsibility and is not shared throughout all levels of the district."

Teachers should be accountable for their assigned responsibilities within the school and system. Paramount among teachers' responsibilities is the provision of high quality instructional opportunities for students. However, it must not be overlooked that each learner must assume the responsibility for his/her own learning. In other words, teachers should, primarily, be held accountable for the processes, not the products, of learning.

Teachers can be held accountable for being informed about student needs and for establishing at least semi-individualized instructional programs to help students attain the stated curricular objectives. In addition, teachers can be held responsible for the selection of learning goals and objectives, for planning and implementing effective strategies designed to help learners reach educational goals, and for avoiding activities which may have an adverse effect on pupils' learning. Accountability must, however, be limited to evaluation of factors which the teacher can produce by his/her own decisions and actions. Accountability for student performance can never be the sole responsibility of the teacher. There are too many other intervening variables which affect student learning. These include innate capabilities of students, environmental constraints, parental contributions to the learning process, the students' own incentives or efforts, as well as numerous other factors beyond the control of the teacher.

Waks[33] mentioned another danger in holding teachers accountable for student performances. He stated, "When the goals are used as the sole point of reference in teacher evaluation, teachers obviously have a powerful motive to sacrifice rich instructional opportunities and to pursue the pre-specified goals to the exclusion of everything else."

In summing up this chapter, it should be emphasized that an attempt has been made to identify several untenable premises of the behavioral objective movement that have tended to cause educators to view CBE programs as being illusionary rather than the remedy for many instructional program difficulties.

The chapter can be considered to be at least partially successful if the reader has fully recognized the following problems:

1. Many educational leaders of the behavioral objective-CBE movements and, subsequently, their followers are strongly divided over the conceptual framework within which they operationally view behavioral objectives.

2. There is current disagreement and lack of understanding on the part of many educators as to what components should be included in a behavioral objective and the role each component should fulfill.

3. CBE programs will be no better than the logic upon which they are conceived and the competencies (goals) and objectives upon which each program is based.

Notes

1. Robert F. Mager. *Preparing Instructional Objectives* (Palo Alto, California: Fearon Publishers, 1962).
2. W. James Popham. *Selecting Appropriate Educational Objectives* (Los Angeles, California: Vimcet Associates, 1967).
3. Ralph W. Tyler. *Report to American Educational Research Association* (mimeographed, n.d.).
4. Frederick Herzberg. "One More Time: How Do You Motivate Employees?" *Harvard Business Review* (January-February, 1968), pp. 53-62.
5. Robert F. Mager. *Goal Analysis* (Belmont, California: Fearon Publishers, 1972), p. 35.
6. Philip G. Smith. "On the Logic of Behavioral Objectives: The Pedagogical Situation Determines Whether Objectives Should Be Precise or Vague." *Phi Delta Kappan*, 53:429-31 (March), 1972.
7. Carter V. Good (Ed.) *Dictionary of Education*, 3rd Edition, (New York: McGraw-Hill Book Company, 1973), p. 262.
8. *Webster's Seventh New Collegiate Dictionary*, G. and C. Merriam Company, Springfield, Massachusetts, 1972, p. 358.
9. Robert F. Mager. *Goal Analysis* (Belmont, California: Fearon Publishers, 1972), pp. 39-40.
10. *Ibid.*, pp. vi, 10.
11. George L. Geis. "Education, Training, and Behavioral Objectives." *Educational Technology*, Vol. 17, No. 5 (May), 1977, pp. 32-36.
12. Robert F. Mager. *Goal Analysis* (Belmont, California: Fearon Publishers, 1972), p. 7.
13. Paul L. Dressel. "The Nature and Role of Objectives in Instruction." *Educational Technology*, Vol. 17, No. 5 (May), 1977, p. 8.
14. Ronald D. Anderson. "Formulating Objectives for Elemen-

tary Science (Part 1)." *Science and Children*, Vol. 5, No. 1, (September), 1967, pp. 20-23.

15. Terrence Piper. "A Synergistic View of Behavioral Objectives and Behavior Modification." *Educational Technology,* Vol. 17, No. 6 (June), 1977, pp. 26-27.

16. H. H. McAshan. *Writing Behavioral Objectives: A New Approach* (New York: Harper and Row, 1970), p. 42.

17. H. H. McAshan. *The Goals Approach to Performance Objectives* (Philadelphia: W. B. Saunders Company, 1974), p. 64.

18. Anita J. Harrow. *A Taxonomy of the Psychomotor Domain: A Guide for Developing Behavioral Objectives* (New York: Longman, Inc., 1972), pp. 3, 100-160.

19. Herbert D. Simons. "Behavioral Objectives: A False Hope for Education." *Educational Digest*: 38:14-16 (April), 1973.

20. Philip G. Smith. "On the Logic of Behavioral Objectives: The Pedagogical Situation Determines Whether Objectives Should Be Precise or Vague." *Phi Delta Kappan*, 53:429-31 (March), 1972.

21. Robert J. Armstrong *et al. The Development and Evaluation of Behavioral Objectives* (Worthington, Ohio: Charles A. Jones, 1970).

22. John A. Thomas. "Behavioral Objectives and the Elephant of Understanding." *Educational Technology*, Vol. 16, No. 12 (December), 1976, p. 35.

23. Robert F. Mager. *Goal Analysis* (Belmont, California: Fearon Publishers, 1972), p. 61.

24. *Ibid.*, pp. 40, 45, 54, 64, 99.

25. H. G. Shane and J. G. Shane. "Ralph Tyler Discusses Behavioral Objectives." *Today's Education*, 62:6 (September-October), 1973.

26. Robert F. Mager. *Goal Analysis* (Belmont, California: Fearon Publishers, 1972), p. 40.

27. Basil S. Deming. "The Performance Approach: Limitations and Alternatives." *The Educational Forum*, Vol. XLI, No. 2 (January), 1977, pp. 213-216.

28. John A. Thomas. "Behavioral Objectives and the Elephant of Understanding." *Educational Technology*, Vol. 16, No. 12 (December), 1976, p. 35.

29. Leonard J. Waks. "Reexamining the Validity of Arguments Against Behavioral Goals." *Educational Theory*, Vol. 23, (Summer), 1973, p. 135.

30. *Ibid.*, p. 141.

31. Basil S. Deming. "The Performance Approach: Limitations and Alternatives." *The Educational Forum*, Vol. XLI, No. 2 (January), 1977, p. 217.

32. Fred C. Niedermeyer and Howard J. Sullivan. "Prospects for School Acceptance of Objectives-Based Instructional Programs." *Educational Technology*, Vol. 17, No. 6 (June), 1977, pp. 22-24.

33. Leonard J. Waks. "Reexamining the Validity of Arguments Against Behavioral Goals." *Educational Theory,* Vol. 23 (Summer), 1973, p. 135.

II.

Introduction to
Competency-Based Education

"The standards of a genuinely liberal education as they have been understood, more or less since the time of Aristotle, are being progressively undermined by the utilitarians and the sentimentalists."

—Irving Babbett

CHAPTER GOALS
The reader should:
1. acquire knowledge of specific terms considered necessary in the overall understanding of competency-based education (CBE);
2. develop comprehension of the contemporary needs of existing experience-based education programs which may be at least partially eliminated through implementation of CBE programs;
3. develop comprehension of the conceptual differences that exist between competency-based education and performance-based education;

4. acquire comprehension of four basic problems of a continuing nature that greatly influence the development of high quality CBE programs.

Most educators recognize that from time to time change is needed. In fact, change is inevitable in educational programs if program quality is to be maintained and improved. Historically speaking, changes have frequently been the result of on-going concern associated with teacher education programs. The competency-based education (CBE) movement is a prime example of one such change that may improve the quality of instructional programs in the nation's public schools and universities.

The long-range promise and, ultimately, the justification of competency-based education (CBE) is to increase student learning by improving the quality of instruction in all schools. Theoretically, this should occur as a direct consequence of improved teacher education programs in the nation's colleges and universities and improved in-service programs for practicing teachers.

A competency-based education (CBE) program is one in which the desired learning outcomes—usually referred to as competencies which represent the specific instructional intents of the program and the behavioral outcomes, sometimes referred to as assessment modes or evaluation indicators—are specified in advance in written form. In addition, each of these components is visibly associated with an instructional delivery system that incorporates an instructional module as its basic component. Thus, the minimum ingredients which must be considered essential in order for a program to be competency-based are (1) the selection of appropriate competencies, (2) the specification of appropriate evaluation indicators to determine success in competency achievement, and (3) the development of a functional instructional delivery system.

Competency-based education must contribute toward the development of superior instructional programs if they are to become any sort of panacea or have any pronounced value for the educational scene. Value in this instance refers to improvement in educational opportunity over that provided by traditional experience-based programs of the pre-behavioral objective era. Experience-based programs can be defined as those requiring students to gain the experiences provided by specifically identified courses in specific areas of study and to achieve some required grade point average in them, the implied assumption being that the student will, at a later date, convert the understandings he or she has developed into useful on-the-job types of performance.

Need for CBE

CBE, in its purest form, has been designed to overcome perennial problems that have plagued experience-based programs prior to the behavioral objective era. These problems were based upon the following needs:

1. *To avoid duplication of content within a program.* A doctoral student graduating from a major university in the south was asked by his major advisor, after completion of all exams, written and oral, "What did you consider to be the biggest waste of your time while pursuing your doctoral degree?" The student, without the least hesitation, answered, "Too much duplication of course content." He went on to explain that in taking Leadership Theory I, Leadership Theory II, Supervision I, Supervision II, and Organizational Theory, he had repeatedly been exposed to the same theories over and over again. This situation can be avoided in CBE programs. The pre-statement of competencies and objectives enables departmental personnel to avoid most content duplication.

2. *To establish and maintain consistency of competencies taught within courses, regardless of the instructor teaching the course.* This involves a form of course proliferation in which teachers may ignore course and catalog guidelines and teach whatever they wish, particularly if they are more comfortable in doing so. The correct use of competency modules requires all instructors to

cover the same content and prevents competency proliferation in which the instructor may teach anything he or she desires or knows.

3. *To improve individualization of instruction.* Many university level faculty members preach individualization of instruction to the teachers they train, but never practice any form of individualization available, such as: (1) content tailored to meet the needs and personal characteristics of a learner; (2) adaptation of content and materials to the learning rates of the students; (3) the presentation of content in self-instructional modules; and (4) the learners' increased choice of the content, objectives, modules, or other instructional materials and resources. Each of these forms of individualization is amenable to CBE programs; however, the greatest advantage is found in the adaptation of content to the learning rates of the students. This is accomplished through built-in recycle opportunities and alternative strategies provided in the instructional modules.

4. *To aid in the refinement of state accreditation practices.* The incorporation of specific competency statements into instructional modules enables the accrediting agency to base its ratings upon specific standards rather than on the global content coverage offered in experience-based or traditional programs.

5. *To revise and implement appropriate systems of evaluation and reporting of student achievement.* In CBE the statement of competencies and their corresponding measures of evaluation or behavioral outcomes in modules helps ensure that the students' success is determined by competency achievement based upon what they know, rather than upon comparisons with what other students know.

6. *To better communicate to the students the learning tasks that they are expected to achieve and how their success will be determined.* In many experience-based programs, the specific content coverage desired and what the learner will have to accomplish in order to demonstrate success has been somewhat of a

guessing game between the student and his or her instructor. Pre-stated module competencies and objectives and their corresponding enabling strategies help students become more fully aware of both their learning tasks, including content and understanding levels, and the demonstrated performance or mastery levels which they will be expected to achieve.

7. *To better provide students with on-going information regarding their personal progress.* The module guidelines and continuous competency assessment and feedback in CBE ensure students of continuous input concerning their achievement and their own personal growth and development. In addition, the instructor profits from being able to utilize this same information in individualizing his or her instruction and in counseling or advising the students.

8. *To better prepare students to function at all levels of learning.* The use of the cognitive, psychomotor, and affective taxonomies to establish the behavioral domain classification levels in the statement of all module competencies helps ensure that various levels of student concept mastery are achieved. This also establishes a basis for determining the behavioral outcomes to be used in post-assessment, since the behavior to be exhibited should be congruent with the level of learning identified in each competency.

9. *To be better accountable to the general public for the educational program standards accepted by educational institutions.* Specific competency statements and objectives outlined in module formats specifically establish the program standards that should apply in judging program accountability after the accreditating agencies and local educational agencies have given program approval. This concept encompasses the idea that all educational personnel, administrators, teachers, and students can be evaluated by the quality of the results they obtain in achieving the objectives for which they have been given accountability. Student success under this plan would be determined by achievement of the objectives to which they are assigned, not by averaging out scores or through standardized testing programs.

10. *To refine certification practices.* Specific competencies, as outlined in instructional modules, will enable teachers to be certified based upon the specific competencies they achieve. Traditional certification practices certify teachers and administrators according to global content areas, such as course numbers, rather than the specifics of what the teachers actually achieved in the courses. Along with the certification refinement, schools can revise their transcripts or add a page to the transcript which states very specifically what competencies a student has achieved. This will allow personnel officers and other administrators to hire employees based upon the specifics of what they know rather than upon general content coverage only.

11. *To provide an efficient means of in-service training and professional development opportunities in order to upgrade the professional competency of all faculty members.* The selection and specification of competencies, the writing of behavioral objectives, and the development of competency modules requires teachers to be better prepared and more up-to-date than was necessary in traditional programs. This is partially due to the increased exposure teachers receive in the circulation of the modules they prepare. In addition, the preparation of the module components along with the overall instructional delivery system helps the teachers to better internalize the content for which they are responsible.

12. *To base a student's fitness to be employed in a given capacity upon his or her demonstrated ability to perform in field situations those functions that are deemed necessary in the positions.* This is perhaps the most overused and overrated statement of the need for CBE by its advocates. Due to its emphasis upon performance behaviors, CBE does cause teachers to become more aware of what behaviors a student should be able to demonstrate in response to competency achievement. However, many competencies are still taught, achieved, and evaluated in classroom situations without the necessity of field station experiences. For example, in teacher education, teachers and administrators are educated in

the processes of comprehensive planning, goal setting, objective specification, curriculum development, development of enabling strategies, and a host of other necessary skills which represent a considerable portion of the work for which they can be held accountable. Yet, these processes are not done in field situations before students.

13. *To better determine student achievement through more systematic procedures of evaluation.* This represents the original and most valid thrust of the behavioral objectives movement. Evaluation of student competency by way of the behavioral outcomes they can exhibit in response to the enabling strategies that have been provided represents one of the finer achievements of CBE. Evaluation represents a *means* for determining success, but one danger has occurred in this area. Many of the behaviorists have attempted to represent evaluation as the *ends* to be achieved rather than the *means* only.

14. *To improve student achievement of desired competencies.* There is not much valid research data concerning student increase in learning that can be attributed to CBE. This is partially because no substantial research and development funds have been made available for this purpose. However, there is an abundance of evidence available that students learn more when they have pre-stated competencies and objectives. This is because they know more clearly what is expected of them and can become more accountable for achieving their learning responsibilities. In addition, the recycling opportunities built into CBE programs may help to further ensure student motivation and effort to become successful (particularly among the slower students).

CBE Versus PBE

Competency-based education has been referred to by many other names, as shown in Figure 2.1.

In each instance that the terminology had been changed, it was in an attempt to clarify the roles of specific programs within the

Figure 2.1. Competency-based education.

context of CBE. CBTE refers to Competency-Based Teacher Education, PBTE to Performance-Based Teacher Education, PBAE means Performance-Based Administrator Education, and PBE represents Performance-Based Education.

Changing CBE to include an additional letter or two in order to better describe the specific role or area of use offers no problem for a program developer. However, replacing the word Competency with the word Performance is misleading and poses a real threat to CBE.

A problem occurs when one requests a PBE advocate to define what he or she means by performance. Usually, the person will answer that performance means one of the following: (1) something that a person can demonstrate; (2) something that can be performed or observed in a field station experience; (3) something that is demonstrated in a manner other than on an achievement test; (4) something performed for which no minimum standard or criterion is available or appropriate; or (5) something which is demonstrated at the higher levels of cognitive achievement and will sometimes involve all three domains.

None of these definitions define performance clearly or adequately enough to erase the confusion in its utilization. One thing does stand out, however, and that is that the advocates of PBE have replaced the concept of *educating students to achieve learning outcomes or competencies stated as goals*, with the concept of *training students to perform behavioral outcomes or performance tasks.*

Geis[1] brought out the difference between education and training and stated that this difference was a fundamental cause for problems associated with the utilization of behavioral objectives. The implication is that the terminal behavior of people who are trained can be described in terms of physical tasks or responses, whereas education, on the other hand, may refer to and/or include situations in which the terminal behavior defies definition.

His point is that the training areas are task and work oriented, but that education is content oriented. Thus, education involves knowledge or understandings which are not the same thing as behavior. He stated that "the final act of a training episode is the execution of the task-relevant behavior" whereas "in education, the actual 'terminal behavior' is called for much less frequently. Usually a sample rather than a complete performance is called for."

Ralph Tyler, considered by many to be the father of the behavioral objectives movement, elaborated further upon the dilemma presented by the training versus educating concept. Tyler's views were expressed in an interview with Fishbein.[2] Tyler suggested that the current emphasis upon performance specificity in the writing of behavioral objectives is due to (1) the success of the business and industrial world in implementing programs involving *management by objectives*, and (2) the success of military and industrial training programs focused upon specific objectives or behavioral outcomes. He further implies that the training approach does not "address the nature of learning and the purpose of education." He stated that "specific learning objectives have often been confused with clear and appropriate educational objectives."

Tyler commented further that a number of educational leaders who appear to be the most impressed by the success of specific skill training programs "failed to distinguish between (1) the learning of highly specific skills for limited job performance, and (2) the more generalized understanding, problem-solving skills and other kinds of behavior patterns that thoughtful teachers and educators seek to help students develop."

This brings up the concepts of "values" and "means." Values can be thought of as being either intrinsic or extrinsic. An essential good that is thought of as being an end within itself and which is sought after for its own sake can be referred to as an *intrinsic good*. A good that is non-essential within itself and is sought after as the means to another good is called an *extrinsic good*.

An *end* is something for the sake of which an act is performed. It is considered to be good in its own right, pursued for its own sake, and has intrinsic value. A *means* is something done for the sake of an end. It is pursued for something distinct from itself and has extrinsic value. Thus, the primary purpose of any instructional program must be to identify and clarify its own ends and intrinsic values.

All instructional programs, competency-based or experience-based, have, at least, the following three major components: (1) the competencies to be achieved, (2) the enabling strategies to be used as means of achieving the competencies, and (3) the evaluation technique that will be employed to determine learner success in achieving the competency.

Competencies represent the cognitive, affective, and psycho-motor learning outcomes established for or by the learner. Frequently, they are referred to as the instructional intents and are stated as goal statements to be achieved. The competencies are the only one of the three components in the educational process that can be considered to be ends and having intrinsic value.

Enabling strategies are designed, not for their own sake, but as a means to aid the learner to achieve his or her competencies. Thus, they are means with extrinsic value. The evaluation component, commonly referred to by many behaviorists as a behavioral objective, represents a behavioral outcome or response a learner can make based upon the level of competency achieved. Evaluation is not valuable for its own sake, but is, primarily, a means to determine the excellence or quality a learner has reached in achieving a competency. Thus, evaluation or behavioral outcomes are means only and have extrinsic value.

It should now be easy to envision the problem established by changing the concept of CBE to a concept of PBE. PBE establishes the evaluation or behavioral outcome as the end with intrinsic value. This is both erroneous and damaging to the overall development and implementation of CBE as a major instructional breakthrough.

In teacher education, some PBTE advocates envision only those performances which place teachers in situations involving student participation as being worthy for use in CBE or PBE. Other CBE educators consider any and all competencies representing desirable student learning outcomes as being important.

Personally, this writer tends to agree with the latter concept. Knowledge is just as important as any other skill, ability, or combination of attributes. Someone once said, "A person can no more perform what he doesn't know than he can come back from where he hasn't been." No skill, ability, or other performance is performed in a vacuum. All complex behaviors are based upon first acquiring knowledge and comprehension. Thus, knowledge and comprehension become essential if more complex performances are to be obtained. The nature of some content areas will determine the level of complexity with which competencies and behavioral outcomes are stated.

There are many competencies which teachers may need to learn that are not performance demonstration or field-based and classroom-oriented. Examples could include learning to write and use behavioral objectives, or the development of skill in using systems analysis techniques. These competencies could be extremely important for teacher use in planning their curricula, but they would never be performed before students. The same is true with many other skills and abilities needed by both students and educators. To assume a program is not performance-based because many competencies do not require field orientation does not appear to be a feasible solution to the problem.

There are at least four ways in which learners can make behavioral outcome responses in CBE. They are by (1) reading what learners write; (2) listening to what learners have to say; (3) observing learner movements or performance demonstrations; and (4) obtaining data requiring some combination of these three response modes.

Many behavioral outcome responses that are possible for learners to perform would not be acceptable to strict advocates of PBTE, but are considered very worthwhile under the CBE concept. Again, we must emphasize that CBE correctly places emphasis upon competencies being intrinsic in value, whereas, PBE places emphasis upon terminal behavioral outcomes.

Continuing Problems in CBE

Use of Behavioral Objective Exchanges or Depositories of Objectives. Shane and Shane,[3] in an interview with Ralph Tyler, asked how he viewed the value or use of depositories of objectives. He answered that they could be useful as a guide. "However, if the objectives are taken mechanically, I think this is as bad as becoming a convert to a religion without knowing what the religion stands for."

The idea of stockpiling lists and catalogues of competencies and/or objectives has been one of the early thrusts of the CBE movement. The current lists and catalogues of outcome, performance-type competencies is appalling. Far too many groups of educators are scurrying around developing lists of competencies which presumably will become the salvation of teachers and teacher educators. Usually, they are arrived at by the consensus of the group compiling the list in each specific instance. In other words, they are situation-specific, and off the top of the heads of the persons comprising whatever group is assembled.

Currently, unless this writer has slept through some very significant discoveries, no satisfactory list exists of crucial skills and behaviors which teachers must utilize in order to perform their assigned responsibilities reasonably well and with satisfaction. It is naive to attempt to perform behaviors that try to define unknown skills and capabilities or to list job competencies that are, in most instances, situation-specific only.

The Florida Catalogue of Teacher Competencies is perhaps a good example and may be the most comprehensive list currently available. This catalogue, funded through the State Department of Education, comprises a list of several thousand competencies which are supposedly necessary for teachers to possess if they are to function effectively.

A casual look at the competency statements in the catalogue reveals that they are not effectively stated with reference to specific competencies. In addition, much-needed criteria for assessment are not available. These competencies, like virtually all other competency lists viewed by this writer, are not sufficient for either classroom implementation or for determining whether or not students actually achieve them. In fact, a more recent study, "The Florida Essential Competency Study," has reduced this list of competencies down to what are referred to as 23 *essential* competencies. These competencies are *also* lacking in the specificity necessary for classroom implementation and evaluation, but could, perhaps, be useful as guidelines in specific situations.

On two occasions, once while attending a meeting at the Florida State Department of Education and again in a telephone conversation with an assistant director of one of the better known behavioral objective exchanges, the writer was told that teachers didn't have the ability to determine their own competencies and objectives. Thus, both groups were advocating that instructional objectives be written for and supplied to the teachers in "cookbook" form.

This concept is revolting and certainly is an insult to the field of education. If teachers cannot perform these functions, it is either because teacher educators have failed in their instruction or because there are shortcomings in the objective-writing approach used. From personal experience, this writer can attest to the fact that teachers can do an excellent job of goal setting, competency identification and statement, and objective specification. In fact, this is the only method for establishing objectives that allows teachers to properly internalize the entire curriculum development process in a manner that is essential for optimum program implementation.

Educational laboratories, as well as universities and research and development centers, have produced many teacher, administrator, and other skills packages; but this writer is unaware of any list, catalogue, or skills package which has been proven to result in greater student learning, whether it be at the knowledge, skill and ability, or student consequence level. To assume that there is any particular set of competencies that supersedes all other competencies in value for teacher education, or any other vocation, and that they retain this value for all people in all situations, is a naive concept at best.

Three additional problems tend to limit the contributions of programs in CBE. These include:

Economic and Political Factors. School systems and universities, in general, are experiencing severe financial difficulties. There is an apparent lack of confidence in educational personnel and programs. This creates distinct problems that, when added to an inflationary economy, have made people wary of many school programs and made them unwilling to tax themselves for school support. The public demands tight control and more accountability for the dollars invested. School bond issues are being rejected with ever increasing frequency and general school program apathy is on the increase. The economic barriers to instructional program funding are closely tied to political barriers. School financing is contingent upon political decisions. By not supporting schools financially, citizens communicate to legislatures that they are dissatisfied. Thus, politics becomes involved in educational program planning. In addition, there are many other special interest groups who compete politically with education for top priority in funding. This is true at both the state and national levels.

Estimates have been made that the current research and development needs of the behavioral objective-CBE movements will require many millions of dollars. It will be difficult to obtain even a small portion of this required financial assistance for R&D within the near future. The lack of financial support can have a severe effect on both pre-service and in-service education programs—a fact that may well jeopardize the behavioral objective and CBE movements.

National Coordination. Before any new instructional movement can be fully operationalized or implemented on a national basis, there must be some effective machinery established that will provide nationwide coordination of work efforts and problem resolution. To operationalize the behavioral objectives-CBE movements, competencies must be identified and stated in specific and valid formats. Instructional delivery systems must be prepared to enable students to better achieve the desired competencies. Assessment systems must be developed to determine program reliability and validity. Many of the current problems already identified by many educators need to be coordinated and resolved before any full-scale implementation of the movement can take place satisfactorily. For example, the controversy over the differences between a learning outcome and a behavioral outcome and the resolution of the problems created by the differences between writing behavioral objectives by the "goals" approach or "outcomes" approach are matters that could be resolved through effective national coordination.

Program Assessment. A multitude of curriculum evaluation models has been submitted over the years. Many of these models have proven to be effective within the context of particular programs and with the objectives that these programs were designed to achieve. In other words, many evaluation models have been effective when viewed on a situation-specific basis. None of the evaluation models can be said to apply across-the-board to all programs. Major assessment problems in CBE include (1) the assumptions upon which CBE is based; (2) the validity and definition of competencies; (3) the certification of student performance of competency; (4) assessment of student progress; (5) assessment of teaching performance; and (6) the development of an adequate technology for performance assessment itself. To date, there appears to be little evidence that any current claims concerning behavioral objectives or CBE, either pro or con, can be supported with irrefutable program assessment evidence.

Summary

In summarizing this chapter, several points can be emphasized. First, it has been shown that competency-based education can make contributions toward solving each of the 14 needs specified in the chapter. Second, PBTE, PBAE, CBTE, and PBE are names often used synonymously with CBE. However, the concept of a program being performance-based rather than competency-based may lead to many problems which can become critical to the life and well-being of the CBE movement. Finally, depositories of objectives, economic and political factors, national coordination, and program assessment are revealed to be continuing problems which can hamper the further development and implementation of optimum CBE progress.

CBE must, in addition to remedying the needs created by experience-based programs, make contributions to at least the three major component areas of the instructional process upon which CBE is founded. That is to say that CBE must aid in: (1) the selection and clarification of appropriate competencies; (2) the specification of meaningful behavioral outcomes to evaluate success in achieving the competencies undertaken; and (3) the development of an efficient and effective instructional delivery system. These three CBE components will be the topics of concern in Chapters III, IV, and V of this text.

Glossary of Key Chapter Terms

Behavioral Outcome: A behavioral response which a learner may perform as an indication of how well he or she has achieved a learning assignment or competency. It is often referred to as a behavioral objective and consists primarily of a demonstrated performance and criteria to indicate how well the behavior must be performed in order to be considered successful.

CBTE: Competency-Based Teacher Education

Competencies: The knowledge, skills, and abilities or capabilities that a person achieves, which become part of his or her being to the extent he or she can satisfactorily perform particular cognitive, affective, and psychomotor behaviors. They represent the instructional intents of a program and are stated as specific goals to be achieved.

Competency-Based Education: An educational program in which the desired learning outcomes or competencies and the behavioral outcomes or evaluation indicators are specified in advance in written form. In addition, each of these components is visibly associated with an instructional delivery system that incorporates a module as the basic component. In these programs, competencies are considered to be ends and to have intrinsic value.

Enabling Strategies: Alternative choices which students may make to acquire the knowledge, skills, and abilities or capabilities set forth in the competencies they are assigned. Normally, these strategies will consist of activities such as reading, listening, interacting, creating, viewing, constructing, observing, and other related activities.

Ends: Those things for the sake of which an act is performed. They are good in their own right, pursued for their own sake, and have intrinsic value.

Evaluation: Behavioral outcome responses used in post-assessment activities to determine whether or not students have achieved assigned competencies. They consist of a demonstrated performance and criteria to indicate the minimum level at which the performance must be executed in order to be considered successful.

Experience-Based Education: An educational program in which students are required to gain experiences provided by specifically identified courses in specific areas of study and to achieve a required grade point average as an indication they have achieved the understandings necessary to perform useful on-the-job types of performances.

Extrinsic Good: An instrumental good that is non-essential within itself and is sought as the means to some other good.

Intrinsic Good: A type of good that is perceived to be essential and is judged worthy of being sought for its own sake or that is considered an end in itself.

Learning Outcome: The competencies, knowledge, skills, and abilities or capabilities that people achieve in an instructional situation which become part of their own being.

Means: Those things done for the sake of an end that are normally pursued for something distinct from itself, and which have only extrinsic value.

PBAE: Performance-Based Administrator Education

PBE: Performance-Based Education. This represents a competency-based education program in which the behavioral outcomes rather than the competencies may be emphasized as ends with intrinsic value.

PBTE: Performance-Based Teacher Education

Notes

1. George L. Geis. "Education, Training, and Behavioral Objectives." *Educational Technology*, Vol. 17, No. 5 (May), 1977, p. 33.
2. Justin M. Fishbein. "The Father of Behavioral Objectives Criticizes Them: An Interview with Ralph Tyler." *Phi Delta Kappan*, September, 1973, p. 57.
3. H. G. Shane and J. G. Shane. "Ralph Tyler Discusses Behavioral Objectives." *Today's Education*, 62:6 (September-October), 1973.

III.

Instructional Competencies

"The school should always have as its aim that the young man leave it as a harmonious personality, not as a specialist. This ... is true ... even for technical schools. ... The development of general ability for independent thinking and judgment should always be placed foremost. ... It is essential that the student acquire an understanding of and a lively feeling for values. ... Otherwise he— with his specialized knowledge—more closely resembles a well-trained dog than a harmoniously developed person."

—Albert Einstein

CHAPTER GOALS

The reader should:

1. acquire comprehension of instructional competencies and the learning format in which they are developed;
2. acquire comprehension of the differences between learning oriented and non-learning oriented goals and how they are established;
3. acquire knowledge of the specific factors which determine a competency's clarity and specificity;
4. develop comprehension of the systematic competency

49

analysis process for establishing appropriate competencies for a unit of instruction.

Competencies are perhaps the most abused component in the triad representing the CBE curriculum development process. An examination of the competency modules distributed by professors of many of the nations largest universities reveals many modules which have no competencies in them, only statements of behavioral outcomes assigned competency status. Research of available literature on behavioral objectives and CBE results in very little explicit definition of competencies or how they should be used and stated.

Many authors and other leading educators are aware of the problems that have occurred in competency development and usage, but few have either the time or specialization of interest to focus upon correcting the situation. Such an attempt will be the focus of this chapter. To the extent that you, the reader, can use the information presented in better establishing your own on-going programs, the author will have been proportionately successful.

A competency should be considered a specific learning task to be achieved by some learner or learner group. As such, it can be conceived as representing a learning outcome consisting of the knowledge, skills and abilities, or capabilities that will become a distinct part of the learner, once it is achieved.

This viewpoint has been well-stated by Gagne[1] in an article in which he contradicted the use of learner behaviors as learning outcomes. He stated:

> The outcomes of learning are sometimes considered simply as changes in behavior; however, this is only part of the story. The changes in student behavior that we gratefully observe imply that persisting states have been acquired. "What is learned" is something new that remains a part of the learner. Some would call these abilities, but I prefer to speak of them as capabilities. ... It is those capabilities that constitute the outcomes of learning.

According to this definition, competencies may be considered to be learning outcomes, learning tasks, or learning intents which can be stated as specific goals. Competencies, as specific goals, represent the ends or intrinsic values upon which a teacher and learner may focus.

Learning outcomes should not be confused with behavioral outcomes. Learning outcomes represent capabilities that are part of the learner; whereas, behavioral outcomes are demonstrations or responses on the part of a learner that he or she has achieved a desired learning outcome or competency.

The Competency Development Theory

McAshan[2] has presented a theory for the learning format in which competencies are developed. This theory is as follows:

Learning theory indicates that learning begins when stimuli (either internal or external) and their reinforcement cause an organism to react. Learning occurs through this process, and the more complex cognitive, psychomotor, and affective motivational systems develop. Thus, all learning can be said to begin when the learner is sensitized to the existence of stimuli. These stimuli may be thought of as occurring from the result of teaching strategies (or enabling activities) that are part of the instructional delivery system in CBE programs.

For the purposes of our present discussion, we will consider all learning as occurring according to a set process or format consisting of two phases, the receiving phase and the internalization phase. The receiving phase consists of four stages—the proprioceptual, preceptual, perceptual, and conceptual. In the proprioceptual stage, a stimulus is picked up by one or more of the learner's primary sensory receptors. This usually involves seeing, hearing, or feeling. These sensory cell receptors transmit stimuli to the central nervous system, referred to as the preceptual stage, which interprets the stimuli and gives further instructions.

From the preceptual stage the stimuli are passed on to the perceptual stage, where a mental image of the stimulus is formed and general awareness takes place. Following this awareness, the stimuli input is passed on to the conceptual stage, which results in thought formulation concerning the stimuli variables. At this point, we might infer that the receiving phase is completed. The proprioceptual and preceptual stages of the receiving phase represent raw input, whereas learning actually begins to take place during the perceptual and conceptual stages of the receiving phase.

The second learning phase, the internalization phase, can be considered as the primary focus of the learning process. This is where the desired learning outcomes occur and are stored. This phase is characterized by the changes that take place within the learner and which become part of the learner. These changes represent the learner's cognitive, affective, and psychomotor development or, in other words, the capabilities that the learner has acquired with reference to understandings, feelings, or movement activities.

These capabilities or acquired attributes can represent many levels of learning that have occurred and are based upon the amount of internalization of feelings, understanding, or movement capability that has taken place. Perhaps the best way to interpret this internalization of learning is through the taxonomies by Bloom *et al.* (1956), Krathwohl *et al.* (1964), and Harrow (1972). Each of these taxonomies portrays several hierarchical levels of capabilities that can be acquired by learners through the learning process.

Figure 3.1 depicts the relationships among learning and the three behavioral taxonomies. It can be assumed that the outcomes of learning should result in the acquisition of capabilities which can be placed into Levels 2.00-5.00 of the affective taxonomy, 1.00-6.00 of the cognitive taxonomy, and 2.00-6.00 of the psychomotor taxonomy.

It should be noted that the learning outcomes are the ends for which all enabling instructional activities are performed. Since the

Figure 3.1. Relationships between learning and the behavioral taxonomies.

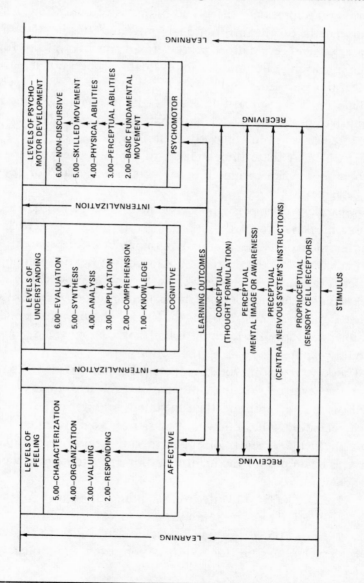

learning outcomes are ends, they may be viewed as having the only intrinsic value to be found in the instructional program. These learning outcomes are the prime purposes of education. All other components of the instructional program, such as the enabling strategies and evaluation processes, are merely means for producing learning outcomes or for evaluating successful achievement of learning outcomes.

One must recognize that learning is never purely affective, or cognitive, or psychomotor, but that the students may develop in all three areas simultaneously. The educator must choose, however, which of these three areas is of primary concern at any particular time when formulating the competencies and/or objectives to be achieved.

Regardless of a person's acceptance or non-acceptance of the hierarchical nature of the taxonomies, it appears safe to say that the learning outcomes defined as the abilities or capabilities that become part of the learner should constitute the competencies which a learner should achieve. Furthermore, most educators will agree that competencies can be placed into one or more of the three domains. Thus, learning outcomes should represent the attainment of specific learning intents or competencies, and these should become the goals of instruction.

The key to writing good competency statements is to determine first the level of learning outcomes that is desired for a specific skill or content unit and then to state it in terms of a specific goal to be achieved. The following two sample goal statements from a unit in PERT (Program Evaluation and Review Technique) can serve as examples for the identification of specific competencies to be achieved:

1. EDA 605 students will acquire knowledge of selected PERT terms and symbols.
2. EDA 605 students will develop the ability to apply PERT techniques in the construction of a functional control network.

Both of these goal statements identify "EDA 605 students" as being accountable for achieving a competency. The term "will acquire" and "will develop" give the goal statements a future time orientation. In other words, they indicate that the desired learning outcome is expected to occur in the future and is not something that students can normally be expected to demonstrate prior to implementaton of their enabling strategies.

"Knowledge" in the first goal statement, and "the ability to apply" in the second goal statement, reveal that the amounts of internalization should be at the knowledge and application levels, respectively, according to the cognitive taxonomy. "PERT terms and symbols" and "PERT techniques in the construction of a functional control network" identify the specific content to be learned.

As soon as a teacher has identified all of the learning outcomes or competencies that are appropriate for a particular unit of study and has stated the competencies in terms of specfic goals, he or she is ready to begin thinking about behavioral outcomes.

Pertinent Literature

There is much support for defining and stating competencies as goals, intents, or learning outcomes. Gronlund[3] supports this concept through his emphasis on understanding as being the purpose of learning, rather than behavioral outcomes which are the responses made after understanding occurs. He states that behavioral outcomes "are simply samples of the types of performance that represent understanding."

Thomas[4] submits the idea that "understanding is a genuine objective of cognitive instruction." He indicates that an objective should be a target or something at which to aim. With reference to the stating of instructional objectives as behavioral outcomes, he states, "I believe they have jumped the tracks of sound educational practice by confusing instructional objectives with the evidence of their attainment." In his summary statements, he suggests that terms like understand can be used to indicate the educational end to be achieved and that they "may be subsumed under goals or unit titles ... that we can conveniently train our instructional shot-guns on."

Harrow[5] states that "Good teachers have always defined their educational goals, tried many different teaching techniques and attempted to evaluate the learning that occurred. These educators saw the behavioral objective movement for what it was—an attempt to communicate more specifically the goals of education in all curricular areas."

In an interview with Fishbein,[6] Ralph Tyler said that an objective does not need to be specific, in terms of the behavioral outcomes model, in order to be clear, attainable, and capable of assessment. Waks[7] suggests that "the teacher should aim at getting the students to understand algebra, not merely be able to do the problems on the final examination." Smith,[8] in disagreeing with the statement of objectives as simply behavioral outcomes, wrote: ... "Stating behavioral objectives is, then, primarily an attempt to increase teaching effectiveness through clarity and mutual understanding concerning goals."

The writing and utilization of behavioral objectives has been adapted from the "Management By Objectives" (MBO) concept introduced by business and industry. MBO is primarily a goal-setting process used to establish a basis for employee accountability for non-learning oriented types of goals and performance tasks.

McAshan[9] has written an account relating the differences between non-learning oriented goals and objectives and learning oriented goals and objectives. Briefly, the following chart will serve as an example.

GOALS

Non-Learning Oriented	Learning Oriented
A. Any goal that is designed to establish the end or focus of an employee's work responsibilities with the ultimate intent of establishing accountability.	A. Any goal that is designed to establish a learning oriented end or focus in order to bring about learner change in cognitive, affective, or psychomotor capability. It can also establish accountability.
B. The goal statement normally identifies *who* is accountable for *what* and *when*.	B. These goal statements will identify a learner or learner group, a learning task consisting of content, and domain identification.
C. This type of goal is converted into a performance objective by the addition of an evaluation component and any necessary conditions.	C. This type of goal statement is converted into a performance objective (behavioral objective) by the addition of an evaluation component and necessary conditions.

Non-learning oriented goals are usually identified through the use of the following goal-setting techniques: (1) Management by objectives, (2) Systems analysis, (3) Task analysis, (4) Needs assessment, and (5) Professional expertise or judgment. The significant point is that in the establishment of non-learning oriented goals, the emphasis is never on content or domain, but upon establishing some type of job responsibility that, in most instances, will not require the "educating" of the employee. In some instances, training will be necessary, but the goals that are set are not for the employee training, but for the job he or she will fulfill upon completion of training.

Learning oriented goals should be designed as a focus for content mastery and the achievement of greater ability to function efficiently at the higher domain levels. Williams[10] defended the position that learning oriented competencies are not the same thing as performance tasks. He stated: "Most tasks required of learners have two components: learning task content and applying generic intellectual operations to that content. ... the learner must first learn, or have previously learned, certain information basic to and determined by the task. For convenience these basics will be referred to as the content of the task."

Based upon the fact that the impetus for the behavioral objective movement was the MBO approach to accountability, it would appear logical that the status and role of the learning oriented goals should be no less important than that of their non-learning oriented counterparts.

Many authors have attested to the value of goals in the development of accountable programs. Riles[11] explained accountability as a process of *setting goals*, making resources available for meeting the specified *goals*, and conducting regular evaluations to determine if the *goals* had been attained. He further emphasized that *goals have intrinsic value* and need to be stated in order to design a relevant evaluation and be accountable for the program being conducted.

Bano[12] said: "Accountability can be defined very broadly to include not only responsibility for performance in achieving *goals*, but, also, for selecting appropriate or relevant *goals* in the first place. Grayboff[13] pointed out, with reference to performance contracts: "the educator sets both the goals and the specific objectives that are to be met through the employment of contracted services ... the district should first state what immediate and long-range *goals* it expects to reach through execution of the performance contract." Lopez[14] stated on the concept of goal setting: "The underlying concept of the goal-setting approach is simple: the clearer the idea you have of what you want to accomplish, the greater your chance for accomplishing it."

Again, it is clear that goals are the ends to be achieved and represent the ultimate values that will accrue as a result of a program's activities. All activities implemented in an accountable program are performed for the sake of either attaining a goal or evaluating to determine program success. It is imperative that this relationship be retained in educational programs and that all educational program activities remain focused upon the ends represented by the educational goals or competencies.

Competency Specificity

Competencies can be broad and general or they can be very specific. It should be remembered, however, that the more specific the target is that we focus upon, the more likely we are to achieve it. In addition, there is an inverse relationship between the level of abstraction at which a competency is stated and the validity of the measurement used to evaluate its achievement. Broad or general goals are amenable to general evaluation, whereas specific goals are amenable to specific evaluation.

Clarity and specificity are essential in well-stated competencies, if they are to become the program's desired ends. Four factors will, in most instances, determine whether a competency does or does not communicate well to its audience. These factors include (1) the identification of the learner or learner group, (2) the classification level of the behavioral domain it is intended to represent, (3) the specific content to be learned, and (4) the statement of future time orientation. Factors two, three, and four together are sometimes referred to as the *learning task*. Factor number one may be omitted for competencies that will be stated in instructional modules. This is because accountability for achieving the competencies will have already been established in another form.

These factors have been adapted from the parent process, Management By Objectives (MBO), which incorporates three factors in non-learning oriented goal statements which are: (1) *Who* will be accountable, (2) for *what* they will be accountable, and (3) *when* the job must be completed.

The first competency communication factor, *learner or learner group*, serves the purpose of assigning who is accountable for achieving the competency. The *learning task*, factors two, three, and four, represent what needs to be achieved. The *domain* establishes whether or not the competency is primarily concerned with cognitive, affective, or psychomotor achievement and the expected level of capability according to the taxonomies edited by Bloom *et al.*[15] and Krathwohl *et al.*[16] and authored by Harrow.[17] The *specific content* refers to the actual content to be learned and later evaluated. *Future time orientation* makes it evident that the learner is not expected to already possess the competency or to be able to demonstrate the competency, but that he or she is to acquire it or to develop the required capability.

Examples illustrating specific competencies in each of the three behavioral domains are as follows:

Cognitive

I. EDA 605 students should acquire *comprehension* of specific terms and related concepts important in the development and understanding of systems and in the use of the systems analysis process.

Communication Critique:
A. Accountable learner group—Students taking the course EDA 605.

B. Learning Task:
   1. Domain—The word "comprehension" places the competency in the Cognitive domain at classification level 2.00. This means that the learning task is intended to help the students develop their skill or ability to make translations, interpretations, and to extrapolate.
   2. Specific content to be learned—"Specific terms and related concepts important in the development and understanding of systems and in the use of the systems analysis process."
   3. Future time orientation—The phrase "should acquire comprehension" indicates that proficiency in this competency is expected to occur at a later date.

II. EDA 605 students will develop the *skills necessary to apply systems analysis techniques* in solving educational problems.

Communication Critique:
A. Accountable learner group—Students taking the course coded EDA 605.

B. Learning Task:
1. Domain—The phrase "skills necessary to apply systems analysis techniques" places the competency in the Cognitive domain at level 4.00 as a minimum. This means the learner will be expected to acquire knowledge and comprehension of systems analysis techniques, be able to make application of these techniques in new problem situations, and will be able to perform analysis level thinking in the process as a minimum requirement of the competency.
2. Specific content to be learned—"Systems analysis techniques in solving educational problems."
3. Future time orientation—The phrase "will develop the skills" indicates that the competency is a learning intent, not something students are expected to perform or demonstrate immediately.

Affective

Teachers in Duval County should develop an *interest* in using behavioral objectives to assist them in the implementation of competency-based education in their own classrooms.

Communication Critique:
A. Accountable learner group—"Teachers in Duval County."

B. Learning Task:
1. Domain—The word "interest" places the primary intent of the competency in the Affective domain. Since interest indicates a very low level of internalization of feeling, the competency could be placed at classification level 2.00. This is the lowest level that a teacher would be expected to use in writing affective competency statements using the affective taxonomy.
2. Specific content to be learned—"Interest in using behavioral objectives."
3. Future time orientation—The phrase "should develop an interest" indicates that the feeling is expected to occur at a later date.

Psychomotor

Tenth grade girls should develop their hip, trunk, and back *flexibility*.

Communication Critique:
A. Accountable learner group—"Tenth grade girls."

B. Learning Task:
   1. Domain—The word "flexibility" indicates classification level 4.00, physical abilities, of the psychomotor taxonomy.
   2. Specific content to be learned—"Hip, trunk, and back flexibility."
   3. Future time orientation—The phrase "should develop" indicates achievement will occur at a future date.

The writer recognizes that there has been more than one effort made in each of the three domains to develop hierarchical or other systems for classifying learning outcomes. Despite these efforts, these taxonomies appear to have received far greater acceptance than any other technique. It is important that this research not be ignored, if teachers intend to become orchestrators of their instructional programs, rather than just fulfill minimum requirements.

The reader should make note that each of the example competencies was specific in regard to a particular learning intent and identified not only the content areas but also the classification level of understanding that would be required of the learner. One might also note that behavioral terms, such as "to demonstrate" or "to perform," were not used in the competency statements. They belong in the behavioral outcome, evaluation, or assessment components of an objective, not in the competency statement.

Since there is more than one approach to writing behavioral objectives, care should be taken not to confuse behavioral outcomes—and the terminology associated with behavioral outcomes—with the requirements of the competency statement. Words such as "to understand," "to appreciate," "to know," etc., which are forbidden as being ineffective in behavioral outcomes, are perfectly good for use in competency statements. Kapfer[18] puts it this way: "strict 'behaviorists' have strongly influenced the behavioral objectives movement to ignore covert behaviors." He sees this as an "unnecessary limitation" and alludes to the fact that objectives should deal "with both overt and covert behavior" . . . "a possible first step in redefining behavior is to agree that invisible mental actions are the basis for voluntary visible behavior."

Competencies and behavioral outcomes should be two different objective components, and the same rules do not apply. This point is well worth repeating. Competencies, hence goals, learning outcomes, or learning intents, are something completely different from behavioral outcomes. Let us say "competencies are peaches and behavioral outcomes are cream." They may fit together on occasion but they don't have the same internal characteristics.

The ingredients required for a competency or goal statement to be specific have nothing to do with the ingredients necessary to a behavioral outcome to become specific. Likewise, behavioral outcome specificity has nothing to do with competency specificity. The only requirement is that whatever behavioral outcome is chosen to evaluate success in competency achievement must be congruent with the intent of the competency.

How abstract or how specific should a competency be? It is possible to develop a course of study with only one global competency statement and several behavioral outcome statements. This error has often been the case during the first ten years of the competency-based education movement. It is also possible to breakdown the global competency statements into a hundred or more sub-competencies, and later behavioral objectives, that are not very meaningful. The global competencies are too abstract, and highly refined sub-competencies are too minute to be practical.

Competencies should be stated at the level of specificity that is the most functional within the context of the content to be learned, the time allotted for competency achievement, and the environmental situation in which it is to be used. In other words, certain realities of the teacher-learner situation will need to be considered in competency development. These realities may include the rationale for the program being developed and the CBE philosophy of the institution, in addition to other factors.

In his interview with Fishbein,[19] Tyler stated: "There are far more good things that children could learn than their time in school permits ... teachers working closely with children often have a notion of the ways in which their students have gained new ways of looking at things, ways of attacking problems, new skills, new interests, and new ideas." He also said that these teachers "can state these kinds of behaviors so that the real meaning will not be lost. Specialists in writing objectives often seem one or two steps removed from actual experiences with children."

Tyler's remarks, not only support the concept of making competencies specific according to the context of a specific situation, but also give additional support to the concept that competencies should be locally derived rather than obtained from pre-stated catalogues or purchased from exchanges or other stockpiles of objective materials.

Competency Setting

Competencies may be obtained from many different goal-setting techniques including needs assessment, limited forms of task analysis, systematic competency analysis, professional judgment and expertise, the theoretical approach, and the textbook analysis approach. Regardless of the approach used, competency writing can become an art and require at least as much specificity and practice in development as does the statement of behavioral outcomes. This fact has become virtually lost in the early rush to learn to write behavior outcome statements.

Competencies are normally based upon some learner need that has been identified and are usually stated as goals to be achieved. The idea is that if the goal is achieved, the need will have been eliminated and the learner will have developed or improved his competence in some desired program area. These goals should be viewed as the educational ends which a learner should obtain from his or her instructional program. Thus, it is easy to extrapolate that care should be taken by the behavioral objective writer to ensure that each competency is appropriate and meaningful, and that it communicates well with its intended audience.

Systematic competency analysis is one good method for selecting competencies for curriculum development activities. This method is similar to systems analysis, but is designed to break down content areas rather than activities or functions. Systematic competency analysis enables large content areas to be reduced to various levels with less abstraction and to determine the specific competencies that would be useful in a given situation.

As an example, let us assume that a graduate course coded EDA 611, Performance Objective Development and Use, is to be taught at a university operating on a quarter system, consisting of eleven weeks of instruction. In addition, we will assume that a competency module will be prepared for use in the course. The first goal or competency to be established would be a broad competency statement and could be referred to as the mission statement. This competency will establish the overall content intent of the course as follows:

EDA 611 Mission Statement
Graduate students in EDA 611 completing this module should acquire the competencies necessary to develop and use performance objectives effectively in carrying out both their instructional and administrative responsibilities.

At this point, the behavioral objective writer will begin breaking down the mission into more specific content by the division process referred to as systematic competency analysis. This involves breaking down the course content into several levels of abstraction. The breakdown will be completed before any of the specific competency statements are written. Competency statements are then developed to achieve the goals as indicated in the final level of the breakdown, which is the level involving the most specificity. In this example, the breakdown could result in the graphic description as shown in Figure 3.2.

Figure 3.2. Course content breakdown.

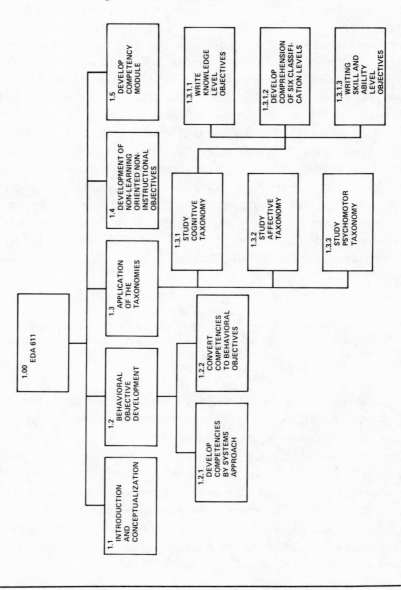

At the completion of. the systematic analysis of the EDA 611 course, competency statements are developed at the final level of analysis for each subsystem. In this instance, competency statements in the form of specific goals will be written for components 1.1, 1.2.1, 1.2.2, 1.3.1.1, 1.3.1.2, 1.3.1.3, 1.3.2, 1.3.3, 1.4, and 1.5. This will result in ten competencies for the course. An example of competencies identified by goal statements for 1.1, 1.2.1, 1.3.1.3, and 1.5 are as follows:

1.1 Acquire comprehension of specific information related to the conceptualization and rationale for developing performance objectives by both the "goals" and "outcomes" approach writing techniques. (2.00)

1.2.1 Develop the ability to write learning-oriented goal statements and to apply a systems approach in the identification of instructional goals. (4.00)

1.3.1.3 Develop the ability to write behavioral objectives at the skill and ability levels of Bloom's *Taxonomy of Educational Objectives: Cognitive Domain.* (3.00)

1.5 Develop the ability to create a competency module for a unit of instruction. (5.00)

Each of these competency statements identifies future time orientation, specific content, and the domain classification level. The accountable learner group was not necessary in the competency statements, because they were identified on the heading page of the module used and again in the mission statement. It should be noted that there is considerable specificity in each of the four competency statements—not the type of specificity demanded by the behaviorists in the statement of behavioral outcomes, but the type that is expected to appear in a competency statement.

Glossary of Key Chapter Terms

Accountability: The assumption of responsibility coupled with the recognition of the authority to whom one is accountable and the assumption that an evaluation will be performed to determine success.

Learning Oriented Goal: Any goal that is designed as an instructional intent and used to help increase a learner's capabilities in the cognitive, affective, or psychomotor domains.

Management By Objectives: A goal-setting process used primarily in business and industry to establish a basis for determining employee accountability for the work assignments for which they are responsible.

Mission Statement: The identification of the overall goal or intent of a total program, course of study, or system being developed.

Non-Learning Oriented Goal: Any goal that is designed to establish the focus of an employee's work responsibilities. (Any goal that does not qualify as a learning oriented goal.)

Systematic Competency Analysis: A competency or goal-setting technique, adapted from systems analysis, that enables a person to break his/her curricular content down into less abstract levels in order to identify specific competencies.

Notes

1. Robert M. Gagne. "Educational Technology and the Learning Process." *Educational Researcher*, January, 1974, p. 3.
2. H. H. McAshan. "Behavioral Objectives: The History and the Promise." *Educational Technology*, Vol. 17, No. 5 (May), 1977, pp. 37-38.
3. N. E. Gronlund. *Stating Behavioral Objectives for Classroom Instruction* (New York: The Macmillan Company, 1974), pp. 4-6.
4. John A. Thomas. "Behavioral Objectives and the Elephant of Understanding." *Educational Technology*, Vol. 16, No. 12 (December), 1976, p. 34.

5. Anita J. Harrow. "The Behavioral Objectives Movement: Its Impact on Physical Education." *Educational Technology*, Vol. 17, No. 6 (June), 1977, p. 32.

6. Justin M. Fishbein. "The Father of Behavioral Objectives Criticizes Them: An Interview with Ralph Tyler." *Phi Delta Kappan*, September, 1973, p. 57.

7. Leonard J. Waks. "Philosophy, Education, and the Doomsday Threat." *Review of Educational Research*, December, 1969, p. 616.

8. Philip G. Smith. "On the Logic of Behavioral Objectives: The Pedagogical Situation Determines Whether Objectives Should Be Precise or Vague." *Phi Delta Kappan*, March, 1972, pp. 53, 429.

9. H. H. McAshan. *The Goals Approach to Performance Objectives* (Philadelphia: W. B. Saunders Company, 1974), pp. 29, 260-301.

10. Reed G. Williams. "A Behavioral Typology of Educational Objectives for the Cognitive Domain." *Educational Technology*, Vol. 17, No. 6 (June), 1977, pp. 39-40.

11. Wilson C. Riles. "Public Expectations." *Proceedings of the Conferences on Educational Accountability*. (Princeton: Educational Testing Service, March, 1971), pp. G1-G5.

12. Steven M. Bano. "An Approach to Developing Accountability Measures for the Public Schools." *Emerging Patterns of Administrative Accountability: A Reader*, L. H. Browder, Jr. (Ed.) (Berkeley, California: McCutchan Publishing Co., 1971), pp. 418-423.

13. Marilyn N. Grayboff. "Tools for Building Accountability: The Performance Contract." *Emerging Patterns of Administrative Accountability: A Reader*, L. H. Browder, Jr. (Ed.) (Berkeley, California: McCutchan Publishing Co., 1971), pp. 418-423.

14. Felix M. Lopez. "Accountability in Education." *Emerging Patterns of Administrative Accountability: A Reader*, L. H.

Browder, Jr. (Ed.) (Berkeley, California: McCutchan Publishing Co., 1971), pp. 418-423.

15. Benjamin Bloom *et al. Taxonomy of Educational Objectives: Handbook One: Cognitive Domain* (New York: Longman, Inc., 1956).

16. David R. Krathwohl *et al. Taxonomy of Educational Objectives: Handbook Two: Affective Domain* (New York: Longman, Inc., 1964).

17. Anita J. Harrow. *A Taxonomy of the Psychomotor Domain: A Guide for Developing Behavioral Objectives* (New York: Longman, Inc., 1972).

18. Phillip G. Kapfer. "Expanding Behavioral Objectives for Educational Design." *Educational Technology*, Vol. 17, No. 5 (May), 1977, p. 16.

19. Justin M. Fishbein. "The Father of Behavioral Objectives Criticizes Them: An Interview with Ralph Tyler." *Phi Delta Kappan*, September, 1973, p. 57.

IV.

Evaluation: Behavioral Outcomes

"Behavior is a mirror in which one displays his image."

—Goethe

"A consciousness of inward knowledge gives confidence to the outward behavior, which, of all things, is the best to grace a man in his carriage."

—Feltham

CHAPTER GOALS
The reader should:
1. develop comprehension of the logic for assigning behavioral outcomes the role of a means of evaluation rather than an instructional end;
2. acquire knowledge of what is meant by congruency in the relationship between learning outcomes and behavioral outcomes;
3. acquire comprehension of the major differences between the "goals approach" and "outcomes approach" behavioral objective writing techniques.

The two quotations at the beginning of this chapter imply one of the basic premises held by this writer—that demonstrated behavior represents only a sample response for the much more significant capabilities that a learner has within himself or herself. Thus, it followed that (1) a person's competencies must be considered to be improvement in one's capabilities, and (2) evaluation to determine success in achievement of competencies should be based upon the sample behaviors a learner can exhibit as evidence that learning has taken place. Geis[1] stated this point in straightforward and simple terms, when he said: "One of the major benefits of producing good behavioral objectives is that one can then produce better evaluation material."

A behavioral outcome, the second major consideration to be made in the triad representing the CBE curriculum development process, is, or should be, thought of as an evaluation or assessment technique. It represents a performance response that a learner can exhibit as evidence that he or she has achieved a desired competency. The behavioral outcome is pursued for something distinct from itself. It is done for the sake of measuring and evaluating whether the learner has or has not been successful in achieving a desired competency. Within this framework, it must be considered as a means rather than an end and having extrinsic value only.

A minor case could be made in support of the behaviorist concept that behavioral outcomes are ends. On the surface, the argument appears to be strong, but it does not seem to stand up under the logic of critical inquiry. In order to examine the logic of this argument, we will need to return to our discussion of goods, with reference to intrinsic and extrinsic ends and means.

The "Summum Bonum" of Education

In the pursuit of all educational endeavors, it appears that one must aim at achieving some good or goods. There may be, however, a wide variation in the goods, termed ends, at which we aim. In education the good may be: (1) knowledge, (2) an ability, (3) a performance for which one receives training, or (4) some purposeful facility beyond either abilities or performances. The value of the end must depend upon how well it represents the highest good attainable in the particular field of inquiry being examined.

Some goods are considered to be intrinsic goods that are essential and are considered to be ends within themselves. These goods are the ultimate goods which are not used directly as means within the framework of their own pursuit. Another group of goods represents extrinsic goods which are non-essential within themselves and are sought as a means to some other good. Finally, there is an in-between group of goods that can be referred to as having both intrinsic and extrinsic value. These goods are usually instrumental ones which, at times, are sought after for their own sake and also find their worth as a means to some other good.

Obviously, all good is good and no good should be considered bad unless it prevents, in some way, the attainment of some higher good or a good that is considered to be the final good and ultimate value toward which we strive. The argument for this is that in education there must be some "*summum bonum*" or highest good achievable in the field or specific area of inquiry. This good would necessarily be something that is sought after for its own sake and not for the sake of any lesser good. Once this good is established, all other activities must be considered to have extrinsic value and be used as means to aid in achievement of this highest good.

The writer submits that there *are* three goods which can be considered to be among the highest goods attainable in education. Roughly stated, these goods are as follows:

(1) *Cognitive.* To develop the ability to understand and think critically, creatively, reflectively, and to pursue problem-solving activities successfully. This means students can: (1) examine evidence and come to conclusions with a high degree of objectivity; (2) use their imagination to explore situations and can plan and communicate with originality; (3) persistently inquire into

life's problems and situations and support or sponsor
evidence that is correct by the nature of its logic; and (4)
discover new relationships in problem-solving situations.

(2) *Affective*. To develop positive attitudes, values, and adjustment toward life and the way it is lived. This includes: (1) the development of emotionalized dispositions that will cause a person to think positively or
negatively toward particular variables; (2) the development of qualities or traits deemed worthy enough to be
socially, morally, and psychologically desirable; and (3)
the adaptation of a person which will enable him or her
to deal more effectively with his or her environment.

(3) *Psychomotor*. To develop the abilities for the human
body to function in a manner that behooves its capabilities. This would include (1) efficiently functioning perceptual abilities that are capable of giving maximum
support in assisting people to function effectually at the
higher levels of the cognitive, affective, and psychomotor
domains; (2) strong and healthy physical abilities to enable a person to function efficiently in all physical and
movement related activities; and (3) movement skills to
increase the range of their basic fundamental movement
activities and to enable persons to enjoy and perform
efficiently reasonably complex movements patterns.

Capabilities in these three areas may not be overtly observable,
but they represent the various capabilities that we strive to achieve
in learning-type situations. They can be considered to be made up
of all of the many competencies that may be developed to increase
a student's level of understandings, feelings or emotions, and
movement activities. We seek to achieve these competencies in
education strictly because that is what "educating" a student is all
about. As these competencies are achieved, the learner is able to
apply them in many situations throughout the course of his or her
life. Significantly, all learning can be placed under these categories,

and no conceivable goal need be omitted when the ends of education are viewed in this manner.

The only place a behavioral outcome can fit into this scale of values is to serve as a means for determining success in competency achievement. No one can deny that with possibly the exception of reflex and basic fundamental movements, behavioral outcomes are performances that could not be executed efficiently, if they were not preceded by learning. It is, likewise, apparent that once learning has occurred, a learner is likely to be able to perform any number of given activities. Thus, the specification of any one performance or small group of performances can serve as no more than just a sample of the responses that the student may be able to make.

These sample behavioral outcomes serve well as overt means of measuring the amount of learning that has occurred. In fact, they are perhaps the only method for obtaining acceptable evidence. They may even be considered to have value inasmuch as in some instances, such as those exemplified by many training programs, the performance may serve as an end. This is particularly true at the lower levels of learning. We have all witnessed trained seals demonstrate the results they have attained through extensive training activities. They are trained well and perform well, but obviously we cannot say they are educated.

In addition to the fact that behavioral outcomes can never be chosen as the highest ends achievable in education and the fact that they can never fulfill the requirements of all contents and domain areas, there are two other problems that result when behavioral outcomes are given the status of ends. First, they prevent the identification of the proper competencies upon which learners should focus, and second, enabling strategies are designed to achieve the behavioral outcomes rather than the true competencies that are stated as goals.

Waks[2] described the behaviorist's orientation as "merely enabling students to answer examination questions in contrast to 'understanding.' " He correctly surmises that this is preposterous. Dressel[3] observed that the behaviorist approach creates severe problems. He emphasizes that this limited approach to defining behavioral objectives prohibits a student from being educated or evaluated for achievement of competencies that do not represent overtly observable products. He further noted that this eliminates "thought, judgment, feeling, creating, and synthesizing except as these are ultimately verbalized or revealed by an observable product....Limiting behavioral objectives to those which are observable essentially eliminates the broad, complex, and cumulative objectives—the truly important educational outcomes—and would replace them by specifics which are somewhat more performance oriented, but little better than rote memorization of content."

Simons[4] gives further support to this concept by his critique on behavioral objectives, in which he criticizes the use of behavioral terms for identifying the goals of instruction. He emphatically states the following points:

> The fundamental problem with this emphasis on behavior is that the crucial distinction between knowledge and behavior is often ignored. The result is a tendency to think about the goals of instruction totally in terms of changing behavior rather than imparting knowledge. No doubt, the emphasis on specific behaviors simplifies measurement, but ... In short, it is not known what, beyond behavior, is being measured....In terms of instructional objectives, the problem is to determine what someone knows by making inferences from his behavior.

Simons further asserts that there is no easily definable relationship between a person's behavior and his or her knowledge. He emphasizes that a person's understanding can find expression in many different behaviors. His remarks are more or less summarized by his statement: "The behavioral objectives movement seems misguided in its zeal to deal mainly in behavior to the exclusion of knowledge."

Congruence Between Learning Outcomes and Behavioral Outcomes

Behavioral outcomes represent the responses a learner can make through use of the abilities or capabilities that have been acquired during the learning process. They may best be thought of as assessment techniques that can be utilized to evaluate whether or not the learner has achieved the desired learning outcomes or competencies that have been prescribed for him.

The difference between a learning outcome and a behavioral outcome can be distinguished easily by reference to Figure 4.1. This figure graphically illustrates the relationships between (1) the learning process which results in learning outcomes, and (2) the responses to learning referred to as behavioral outcomes.

Close inspection of Figure 4.1 reveals that there should be a match between the learning outcomes or competencies that a learner is to achieve and the behavioral outcomes that are chosen as indicators of success in competency attainment. For example, if a goal is established for the achievement of a competency at the application level, Level 3.00 of the cognitive domain, then the behavioral outcome chosen as an indicator of successful competency achievement should also require a response at the application level. A competency stated at Level 5.00 would likewise require a behavioral outcome or response at Level 5.00 in competency assessment.

This same relationship exists between the learning outcomes in all three of the domains according to the hierarchical order portrayed in the cognitive, affective, and psychomotor taxonomies. In other words, there should always be congruence between the learning intent or learning outcome and the behavioral response or behavioral outcome that is used to evaluate success in achieving the desired learning.

Behavioral outcomes are stated as specific performances, behavioral activities, or assessment instrumentation that learners will successfully achieve as an indication that learning has occurred.

Figure 4.1. Relationship between learning outcomes (learning) and behavioral outcomes (responding).

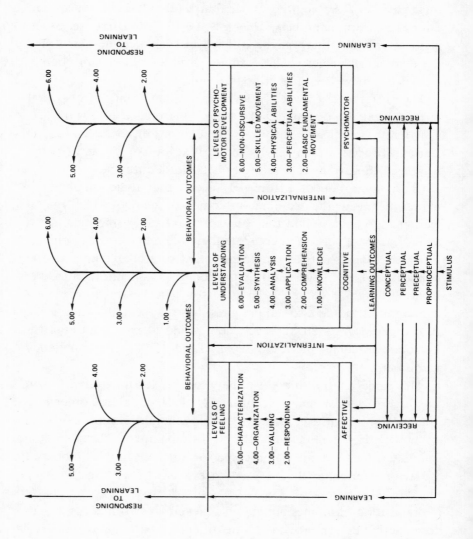

In addition, a criterion is established to indicate how well the assessment activity will need to be achieved. Possible behavioral outcomes to assess student achievement of the competencies previously stated on page 54 in Chapter III under the Competency Development Theory might be as follows:

1. Given a 20 item objective short answer and multiple choice test, consisting of 12 selected PERT terms and eight PERT symbols, the students will select the best response or fill in the correct response with 80 percent accuracy.
2. Given a PERT activity chart including a list of predecessor and successor events, the description of their corresponding activities, the average expected elapsed time for each activity, and a beginning date, students will correctly develop a written PERT control network without error in any of the data used to graphically illustrate the networks.

These two relatively simple behavioral outcome statements each contain a required performance and a criterion. In the first example, the written test is the performance, while "achieving 80 percent" correct answers is the criterion. In the second example, developing a written PERT control network is the performance, whereas "doing so without error" is the criterion. One must note that these behavioral outcomes do not indicate why they are being done, what goal they will achieve, or the specific level of internalization of understanding that is being required. They are actually assessment behaviors which must be matched with the previously stated competencies before their value can be established.

Once an educator understands that the learning outcomes or competencies are not the same thing as the behavioral outcomes (which are usually one-time observations of behavioral responses), he or she must question the value of any behavioral objective that is stated as a behavioral outcome only. This problem has caused more teacher frustration and has imperiled the behavioral objectives movement perhaps more than any other one factor.

Congruence in the behavioral outcome includes agreement be-

tween the desired competency or goal and the evaluation outcome performance in respect to domain, classification level, content, and other indicators. Since the behavioral outcome to be used is merely one of a variety of alternatives for evaluating success in achieving a competency, it is a real challenge for the behavioral objective writer to select, insofar as possible, a behavioral outcome with a performance and criterion that matches the competency or goal statement completely.

Good communication is essential in almost any educational endeavor. Behavioral outcome statements may well include givens, conditions, and other optional statements, in addition to the performance and criterion, in order for the objective being written to communicate more effectively with its intended audience. The outcome performance component of a behavioral outcome requires far better description than just the use of simple verbs such as "to identify" or "to demonstrate" some variable. What specifically is the student going to be doing when he or she identifies or demonstrates?

If Paul Revere had only been informed that the watchman would "identify" or "demonstrate" which way the British were coming, he would have wondered what that foolish man was doing up in the tower of the old North Church swinging lanterns. The behavioral outcome used in this instance, however, included in the performance statement the swinging of the lanterns and a criterion of "one if by land and two if by sea." This information was properly communicated to Paul Revere and history records the results.

Another way to view the value of a behavioral outcome or assessment technique is to ask yourself the question as to whether or not you ever apply assessment techniques or evaluation measures to anything purely for the sake of the information obtained. No, you will find it is always for the purpose of making a decision about something distinct from the value of the observation itself. Another criterion you may use is to ask yourself whether or not the tests or other performance demonstrations you administered to your students last year have any real or useful value to them today. Again, the answer is no! The performance they gave may have helped you evaluate their progress, but only the knowledge or learning outcome, or competencies that they developed and have retained, are still of value to them.

The Goals Approach to Using Behavioral Outcomes

Behavioral outcomes are perhaps best used when stated in conjunction with, or as part of, the specific competency they have been designed to assess. This will: (1) aid in retaining the value of the competency as being the desired end, (2) assist in retaining the value of the behavioral outcome as being an assessment mode, and (3) aid in establishing congruence between the two components. This technique will better insure that educational goals will become operational rather than eliminated or downgraded.

Deming[5] thinks that the operationalization of educational goals is possible. On this point, he stated, "We have evidence that such a distinction has not been overlooked by all practitioners of the performance approach. Particularly noteworthy in fostering this distinction are texts by Gagne and Briggs[6] and by McAshan."[7] Deming refers to this objective-writing approach as one method that helps distinguish between learning of specific skills for limited job performance and the more generalized understandings and problem-solving skills that thoughtful teachers help students to develop.

Many of the recognized problems of behavioral objective development and use can be eliminated by writing behavioral objectives by McAshan's "goals approach" technique. In this approach, behavioral objectives are viewed as having two components which include a goal (competency) and the behavioral outcome that will be used to evaluate success in achieving the goal.

The two example cognitive competencies stated previously in Chapter III under Competency Specificity can serve as examples that illustrate the conversion of competency statements into behavioral objectives by the addition of behavioral outcomes.

EDA 605 students must:

A. Acquire comprehension of specific terms and related concepts important in the development and understanding of systems and the use of the systems analysis process. *Success will be evidenced by an eleven item written examination (consisting of terms to be defined, completion and true-false questions), on which they will achieve at least nine correct answers.*

B. Develop the skills necessary to apply systems analysis techniques in solving educational problems. *Success will be determined by their demonstrated ability to correctly perform systems analysis processes in the development of a written management plan designed to solve a specific problem you have identified. The criteria to be used by the professor in evaluation of the management plan consists of:*

 1. The adequacy and appropriateness of the mission, introduction and/or rationale and philosophy statements with regard to application of the specific problem you have identified for solution.

 2. The appropriateness and quality of the performance objectives developed to specify "what needs to be done." Particular emphasis is placed upon the statement of overtly observable measures of evaluation.

 3. The creative relationships (or "goodness of fit") between the identified subsystems, subsystem components, interim components, and tasks and the mission of the system.

 4. The overall quality of the system produced (as evidenced by the person's or group's ability to follow the six guideline steps for development of the system) and the creative ingenuity and functional utility displayed in developing a graphic description of the management plan.

 5. Group assessment of each individual's contributions toward development of the completed system by use of a peer-group-rating form.

It is easy to see that each of these objectives has two components—the competency or goal to be achieved and a behavioral outcome to determine success. Each behavioral outcome has a specific performance (written examination and written management plan) and specific criteria to be used as the minimum standard for success (nine correct answers and five stated criteria to be used by the professor in evaluating the management plan). These two illustrations also indicate that behavioral outcomes can be very simple, such as in the first objective, or more complex, as shown in the second. The objectives also reveal that the format for adding behavioral outcome statements to competencies may be flexible.

In the goals approach to writing performance objectives, the behavioral outcome is never stated alone. This is because it has no real value except when used in conjunction with the end it serves. There are several important advantages to writing objectives by this approach.

First, this writing process makes clear that the learning intent or understanding to be achieved is the competency or goal, not the behavioral outcome. Second, it enables both the objective writer and the intended audience to better examine the behavioral outcome to be sure it is appropriate and congruent to the competency it is designated to define. Thirdly, and most importantly, it better assures the teacher of planning program strategies, materials, and activities designed to achieve the competency, not the behavioral outcome. Finally, it aids the teacher or professor in revising both his or her statements of competencies and behavioral outcomes from time to time.

Gronlund[8] alluded to the same concept. He recommended first writing the "general instructional objective" (goal, competency, or desired understanding) and then listing a sample of the specific behavior that one is willing to accept as evidence of the attainment of that understanding. Gronlund's writing technique can also be classified as a type of "goals approach." Conceptually, it is very similar to McAshan's[9] "goals approach" inasmuch as he envisions each objective as consisting of two parts—the general instructional objective (competency or goal) first and then specification of the specific evaluation behaviors. He states, "This procedure makes clear that the instructional objective is understanding and not defining, identifying, or distinguishing between things. These latter types of behavior are simply samples of the types of performance that represent understanding."

This technique conceptualizes an objective quite differently from that presented by the behaviorist users of the "outcomes approach." Gronlund[10] emphasized that behavioral outcomes serve only as samples of behavior that one is willing to accept as evidence that the general instructional objective (goal or competency) has been attained. He further states, "Our teaching efforts must be directed toward the general objectives of instruction and not toward the specific samples of behavior we have selected to represent each objective."

Despite the validity of Gronlund's[11] behavioral objective conceptualization and writing technique, it is unfortunate he chose to name the first component of his objective "the general instructional objective." This has resulted in many educators failing to understand the conceptual difference between Mager's[12,13] works and that of his own. Some people have equated "general instructional objective" to mean the same thing as Mager's[14] broad, global, abstract, goal.

Armstrong, Cornell, Kramer, and Roberson[15] of the EPIC Evaluation Center, Tucson, Arizona, developed an Organizational Structure of Variables which resulted in an approach to writing behavioral objectives that utilizes characteristics similar to the "goals approach." They specify that each objective should consider six variables or elements in order to make the objective more precise and useful for evaluation purposes. The elements are:

"1. Institutional variable (student, teacher, etc.)
2. Instructional variable (content, etc.)
3. Behavioral variable (cognitive, etc.)
4. Measurement (tests or method, etc.)
5. Time needed (one year, etc.)
6. Proficiency level (grade equivalent, etc.)"

Although the EPIC technique does not describe objectives as having two components (goal and evaluation), the institutional, instructional, and behavioral variables can be translated as being the learner, content, and domain in the goal statement of the "goals approach." In addition, measurement, proficiency, and time needed are similar to the performance, criterion standard, and optional statement found in the "goals approach" evaluation component.

The Outcomes Approach to Using Behavioral Outcomes

Historically speaking, Ralph Tyler, a leader in educational evaluation and research, is generally given credit for the current emphasis on the idea of writing behavioral objectives. He was evidently concerned with improving the writing of goal statements so that they would become more functional. Much later, the behavioral objective movement began to take hold with the assistance of the Mager[16] text, *Preparing Instructional Objectives*, and the filmstrips prepared by Popham[17] and his Vimcet Associates.

This book and the filmstrips served as catalytic agents in the promotion and conceptualization of the behavioral objective movement. At first, the materials appeared to offer a simple solution to the concerns of Tyler. However, along with the instructional boom which was created by the use of these materials, there appeared current problems which have become so deeply embedded in the behavioral objective and CBE movements that they could eventually destroy both, unless their shortcomings are recognized.

The innovative work and instructional materials developed by these two pioneers of the behavioral objective movement provided instruction in what can be referred to as the "outcomes approach" to writing behavioral objectives. Under the outcomes approach, behavioral objectives are defined as a performance or behavioral activity expected from a learner, a criterion by which the performance can be judged to be successful, and any givens or conditions that are necessary for the performance to occur satisfactorily. Two examples of behavioral objectives written by the "outcomes approach" technique are as follows:

1. Given the proper equipment upon which to perform, each girl will increase by at least three the number of squat thrusts performed during one minute.

2. Given instruction and practice opportunities, two days a week for a period of eight months, seventy-five percent (75%) of the students will be able to bend forward from a standing position and lay the palms of the hands flat on the floor, keeping the feet together and legs straight for a 15-second interval.

The required performance, criterion, and givens are obvious in each of these objectives. One does not, however, know what the purpose of the performance is or what population of students the objectives are intended for. Enabling instructional strategies will be prepared primarily to achieve these performances. No one other than the person who wrote the objective can tell that the real, desired competencies or goals of the two objectives were: (1) to improve agility of seventh grade girls, and (2) for twelfth grade gymnastic students to increase body suppleness as defined by measured trunk-hip flexibility. This approach implies that there is no difference between the goals of instruction and the desired behavioral outcomes that are to be used to determine success in achieving the goals. Taken one step further, this means that, since goals are merely thought of as broad, abstract statements of intent, they are better defined by specific behavioral outcomes. This implies that there is no difference between a behavioral outcome which is designed to assess competency achievement and the competency itself.

The best way to emphasize the differences that exist between the "outcomes approach" objectives advocated by the behaviorists and those stated by the "goals approach" techniques is to take three simple objectives representing the cognitive, affective, and psychomotor domains and to state them by both the goals and outcomes approach techniques. This will make it possible to better envision the problems that do occur in objectives stated by the "outcomes approach."

Cognitive

Outcomes Approach: Given an opportunity to select a mission goal, the student will demonstrate his or her ability to correctly break the mission down into a written management plan that meets the requirements of each of four evaluation criteria established by the instructor.

Goals Approach: EDA 605 Students must develop the ability to apply systems analysis techniques to problem-solving. Success will be evidenced by their demonstrated ability to correctly perform systems analysis processes in the development of a written management plan designed to solve a specific problem they have identified according to each of four criteria established by the instructor.

Psychomotor

Outcomes Approach: Given ten building blocks, each child will be able to place by shape eighty percent (80%) of the blocks into their correct categories.

Goals Approach: Preschool children should develop the abilities of visual acuity and prehension movement so that when given ten building blocks, each child will be able to place by shape eighty percent (80%) of the blocks into their correct categories.

Affective

Outcomes Approach: Fifty percent (50%) of the seniors will seek out opportunities for actual involvement in one current problem or social issue that affects their own community.

Goals Approach: Twelfth-grade American History students should become committed to appropriate current social, economic, and political problems that affect their own community as evidenced by fifty percent (50%) of seniors seeking out opportunities for active involvement in one current problem or social issue that affects their own community.

It is easy to see both the functional and conceptual differences between these two objective-writing approaches in each of the examples stated. First, each of the goals approach objectives identifies a specific purpose, competency, or instructional intent, such as (1) the ability to apply systems analysis techniques, (2) abilities of visual acuity and prehension movement, and (3) commitment for appropriate current problems. The outcomes approach objectives do not specify any purpose, but only specify the behavioral outcomes that will be accepted as evidence that some unknown learning or competency has been achieved.

The outcomes approach objectives limit their uses to only one possible method of determining success; but by identifying the instructional intent first in the goals approach, the behavioral outcomes can be changed to many other performances to indicate success, if such performances are found to be more appropriate.

Perhaps the biggest advantage of the "goals approach" objectives, as stated, is that strategies will be developed to achieve the competencies of (1) applying systems analysis techniques, (2) visual acuity and prehension movement, and (3) commitment for appropriate current problems. In contrast, the outcomes approach-stated objectives only permit the preparation of strategies to (1) develop a management plan, (2) place blocks into their correct categories, and (3) seek out opportunities for involvement in social issues. In other words, the goals or competencies are the desired ends under the "goals approach," and the behavioral outcomes are the desired ends under the "outcomes approach." Each approach develops strategies to achieve whatever they view to be the desired ends.

In summing up behavioral outcome statements, one must admit that emphasis on properly stated behavioral objectives has improved teacher evaluation practices. This is not to say that we can evaluate better by new means, or in ways different from those used prior to the behavioral objectives era. Evaluation has improved because more specific competencies have been identified and because more emphasis has been placed upon evaluation data.

While diversity and originality are highly desirable in various fundamental changes that take place in the field of education, beyond a certain point they represent an acute liability. Due to its early development in the behavioral objectives movement, there are still many more users of the "outcomes approach" than there are users of the "goals approach." This, however, speaks to number, not quality. The dictionary states that a goal is "an end toward which work effort is directed." Instructional goals are learning intents specifically defined as competencies, not behavioral outcomes. Persons seeking an answer to the behavioral objectives definition question should base their conclusions upon the worthiness of the operational definition they use, not on the number of users. A competency or goal statement by itself lacks the behavioral outcome necessary for operationalization. An evaluation or behavioral outcome by itself lacks a purpose. By placing both components together as one statement, both shortcomings are eliminated.

Glossary of Key Chapter Terms

Goals Approach Objective-Writing Technique: An approach to writing behavioral objectives that requires a specific statement of a competency, or goal, in addition to a behavioral outcome to be used for purposes of evaluation.

Outcomes Approach Objective-Writing Technique: An approach to writing behavioral objectives that requires no statement of competency, but only the statement of a behavioral outcome that includes a behavioral performance and a criterion standard. Does not require competency identification.

Summum Bonum: The highest good achievable.

Notes

1. George L. Geis. "Education, Training, and Behavioral Objectives." *Educational Technology*, Vol. 17, No. 5 (May), 1977, p. 35.

2. Leonard J. Waks. Philosophy, Education, and the Dooms-day Threat." *Review of Educational Research*, December, 1969, pp. 607-621.

3. Paul L. Dressel. "The Nature and Role of Objectives in In-struction." *Educational Technology*, Vol. 17, No. 5 (May), 1977, p. 9.

4. Herbert D. Simons. "Behavioral Objectives: A False Hope for Education." *Educational Digest*, 38:14-16 (April), 1973.

5. Basil S. Deming. "The Performance Approach: Limitations and Alternatives." *The Educational Forum*, Vol. XLI, No. 2, (January), 1977, p. 214.

6. R. M. Gagne and L. J. Briggs. *Principles of Instructional Design* (New York: Holt, Rinehart, and Winston, Inc., 1974).

7. H. H. McAshan. *The Goals Approach to Performance Objectives* (Philadelphia: W. B. Saunders Company, 1974).

8. Norman E. Gronlund. *Stating Behavioral Objectives for Classroom Instruction* (New York: The Macmillan Company, 1974), pp. 4-6.

9. H. H. McAshan. *The Goals Approach to Performance Objectives* (Philadelphia: W. B. Saunders Company, 1974).

10. Norman E. Gronlund. *Stating Behavioral Objectives for Classroom Instruction* (New York: The Macmillan Company, 1974).

11. *Ibid.*

12. Robert F. Mager. *Preparing Instructional Objectives* (Palo Alto, California: Fearon Publishers, 1962).

13. Robert F. Mager. *Goal Analysis* (Belmont, California: Fearon Publishers, 1972).

14. *Ibid.* p. 35.

15. Robert Armstrong *et al.* "A Scheme for Evaluation." In *Educational Accountability Through Evaluation* (Englewood Cliffs, New Jersey: Educational Technology Publications, 1971).

16. Robert F. Mager. *Preparing Instructional Objectives* (Palo Alto, California: Fearon Publishers, 1962).
17. W. James Popham. *Selecting Appropriate Educational Objectives* (Los Angeles, California: Vimcet Associates, 1967).

V.

The Instructional Delivery System

"The highest function of the teacher consists not so much in imparting knowledge as in stimulating the pupil in its love and pursuit."

—Amiel

"The secret of successful teaching is to teach accurately, thoroughly, and earnestly; this will impart interest to instructions, and awaken attention to them."

—C. Simmons

CHAPTER GOALS
The reader should:
1. acquire comprehension of the major components of an instructional delivery system as it applies to competency-based education;
2. develop the ability to design his/her own competency module format for a unit of instruction.

The instructional delivery system is the third major area of concern in the triad representing the curriculum development process

93

of CBE. The instructional delivery system refers to all of the human, material, and other resources, activities, and strategies that are designed to help students acquire mastery of the competencies to which they are assigned. It is a key component in the development of any CBE program and helps ensure program flexibility by enabling each teacher to do his/her "thing" with reference to teaching.

Curriculum development is usually concerned with the identification of appropriate competencies, placing them in logical sequence, and converting them into behavioral objectives. CBE emphasizes the point that the teacher is the most important factor in the teaching-learning process. In most instances, the teacher will identify the competencies, determine what behavioral outcomes will be appropriate for evaluating competency achievement, and then plan and implement the entire instructional delivery system, including an "instructional competency module."

It is the module, more than any other single item, that assists the teacher in bringing CBE into focus in the most meaningful manner for both the student and the teacher. A module serves as: (1) a written guide to direct the learning efforts of individuals or groups of students, (2) a teaching plan for the instructor, and (3) an in-service training tool for faculty professional development activities. Instructional modules may be developed under many different formats and may include a variety of components.

There are several factors to be considered in module development. First, students who are going to study from several different modules should not be required to use modules with radically different formats and styles. Second, faculty members should agree in advance on the definition of competencies and behavioral objectives and the roles they will serve in instructional modules, so that students are not confused when changing from one module to another. Third, modules should be coded for good communication as an aid in storage, distribution, and use. Finally, they should not be overly complex.

It should be remembered that the chief values of a competency module lie in: (1) the identification of competencies, (2) the statement of corresponding behavioral objectives, and (3) relating these components to representative enabling strategies. All of the remaining module components are developed only as a means to effectively implement these three.

Occasionally, modules are developed as learning packets that are considered to be self-sufficient and suitable for individualized instruction or independent study purposes. These learning packets can be effective, but may create problems of: (1) flexibility, (2) cost, (3) copyright violations, and (4) limited content coverage. Perhaps the best competency modules, in the long run, are those that are the easiest to operationalize and to revise for improvement.

Although no one format can be considered best for everyone, the author does propose the following format that has been proven to be effective in the College of Education at the University of North Florida. Anyone wishing to do so may use it as a type of guideline that can be modified to fit the needs of his/her own program and student requirements. The reader should keep in mind that this module format is not intended to be primarily used as an independent study guideline. Student-professor interaction is expected at regular intervals.

Module Format and Components
I. *Heading Page*
The heading page may be used to communicate the following types of information:
   A. University Name
   B. College of Education
   C. Department Name
   D. Course Title
   E. Coding (Course Number)
   F. Prerequisites

G. Date Developed or Revised

H. Student Information

    (1) Name

    (2) Address

    (3) Phone

    (4) Student Number

    (5) Price

    (6) Other(s) according to local situation

In some instances, the heading page may be color coded and could consist of two pages with a window-like opening in the first page that focuses upon specific information. This will allow a school to develop modules that are distinctly unique and bear both the school colors, name, and seal on the front cover sheet.

II. *Mission Statement or Mission Objective*

The mission statement identifies the overall goal or intent of the module being developed. It broadly outlines the program focus or overall area for which specific competencies and interim performance objectives will be stated. How success in achieving the mission or overall competency will be determined may also be included at the discretion of each faculty member. In this event, the mission statement becomes a mission objective.

III. *Operational Definitions*

Any word used within the module being developed which may be abstract or misleading in the way it is to be used should be defined. This does not warrant the definition of a term to mean whatever you want it to mean, but it does enable the module developer to limit its meaning or to bring the meaning into proper focus.

Operational definitions include those words which appear to be ambiguous, which have confusing interpretations, and which can make a difference in the student's understanding of their use in the module. Normally, there should be no need to operationally define more than a few words.

IV. *Introduction or Rationale*

The purpose of this component is to introduce the student to the content of the module and to provide him/her with an overall view of the reasons underlying the study of that particular content.

V. *Instructions (Operational) for Utilization*

Each module should attempt to be very clear in regard to the processes students will use in proceeding through it. Thus, every module should have its own set of specific instructions which outline the steps necessary to complete all learning tasks.

VI. *Evaluation and Grade Reporting*

A school's Academic Standards Committee usually requires each student be assigned a grade for each course he/she attempts. Grades usually are reported as A, B, C, D, F, or I. Since each student will be required to achieve specific competencies as outlined in the course module, he/she has a right to know—in advance—how his/her grades are to be determined. Thus, this modular component should clearly communicate the basis upon which students will be evaluated and grades reported.

VII. *Statement of Specific Competencies*

Competencies, which represent the specific learning intents or goals to be achieved by the students, should be stated sequentially at this point. These learning intents, which represent the long-range ends or learning outcomes to be achieved by the student, should not be confused with the behavioral outcomes (performance, criteria, givens, and conditions) which will later be included as indicators of competency achievement.

It should be kept in mind that these competency statements represent the standards that are required for state accreditation. They can be considered to be the more specific sub-goals stated within the constraints of the mission objective or terminal performance competency. During the accreditation visits by various agencies, they can be listed to represent the College of Education's competencies or standards. Since the competencies have not yet been achieved when students encounter their modules, they should be stated with a future time orientation, rather than as exit statements.

VIII. *Interim Objectives, Enabling Activities, Learning Resources, and Post-Assessment Statements*

A. *Interim Objectives*

These interim behavioral objective statements represent extensions of the specific competencies identified in Section VII. They include, in addition to the competency statement, the behavioral outcomes expected from the learner as an indication of his/her success in having achieved the desired competencies. The behavioral outcomes component may include the performances, criteria, givens, and conditions necessary for the instructor to determine success.

There should be one interim objective for each competency stated in Section VII. In addition, each behavioral outcome should represent a congruent relationship between the required competency and the necessary evaluation data that will determine success.

The interim objectives can be stated by restating the specific competency and attaching the behavioral outcome statement or evaluation component. The advantages of this method are to (1) retain focus on the competency as the desired end, (2) aid in visual interpretation of the congruence between the competency and its behavioral outcome or evaluation requirement, and (3) keep the student from having to constantly refer back to the pages upon which the specific competencies are stated in order to associate the required behavioral outcome with the competency or purpose for which it has been stated.

Each interim objective should be stated on a separate page along with its own enabling activities, learning resource statements, and post-assessment statements. This format will allow for easier future revision of the module's objectives. An objective can be revised merely by pulling out the page or pages to be changed without affecting the following pages.

B. *Enabling Activities and Learning Resources*

This section designates the alternative choices from which students may choose to acquire the knowledge or skills identified in the competency statements. The enabling activities and learning resources statements for each interim objective should follow immediately after the corresponding objective statement to which they apply. The learning resources may include any human and material resources necessary for competency achievement.

These instructional strategies, as well as the learning materials and resources necessary to implement them, are specifically selected by the individual instructor as a guideline for competency achievement. Some students may attempt to achieve selected competencies by independent study; thus, the recommended instructional choices at their disposal need to be clearly and concisely stated.

C. *Post-Assessment Statements*

These statements are placed after the listing of activities and learning resources for each interim performance objective. The purpose of these statements is to further clarify the objectives by providing supplemental information concerning each objective to be achieved. These statements are particularly useful as an aid in helping to communicate more fully the evaluation component of an objective. Objectives will normally be precise statements of learning intents and/or outcomes. Frequently, additional information is needed for the student to fully understand all of the requirements of an objective.

This information may include (1) further identification of the criteria by which the objective will be evaluated for success, (2) a more detailed description of the behavioral outcome expected, (3) clarification of the learning classification level at which the objective will be evaluated, and/or (4) information providing any additional data deemed necessary by the module developer.

Another use of the post-assessment statements can be to explain the number, type, and conditions of the recycle activities to which the learner will be entitled. Imaginative use of this modular component can prevent much misunderstanding on the part of the student.

IX. *Appendix*

This is not to be considered as an essential part of any module but can be included at the discretion of the individual faculty member. Faculty members must be careful about plagiarism in the development of modules. It may be best to use some materials as handouts rather than build them into the module or include them in the appendix without approval. References can be made to reading assignments when there is doubt concerning the use of copyrighted material. In the event that pre-assessment activities are necessary, the documentation may be included at this point.

Module development should include all components that are necessary for a learner to achieve the purposes for which the module is prepared. In reality, it is not the rigid following of any set of module guidelines or format that produces the most efficient module. It is the module developer's ability to select his/her own module ingredients and to synthesize them in a manner that best serves his/her own and his/her students' interests that is essential. Appropriate competencies, how competency attainment will be evaluated to determine success, and an adequate selection of enabling strategies are the only essential components that must be utilized.

A competency module utilizing each of the module components outlined in this chapter is shown in the Appendix at the end of this text. The author has used revised versions of this example module with considerable student success over a six-year period extending from 1972 to 1978.

Enabling Strategies

Enabling activities or strategies are considered to be the number one concern of the instructional delivery system. They refer to the carefully developed plan or methods that a teacher will devise and employ as a means of enabling students to gain the ends which they seek. The ends in this instance refer to the specific competencies which have been pre-stated.

A significant difference between the value of enabling strategies and that of competencies is that strategies serve as a *means* only. In other words, strategies are not valuable for their own sake, but are done for the sake of the ends. Since they are pursued for reasons distinct from any value of their own, they have only extrinsic value. The same is true for the entire instructional delivery system.

The development of strategies is one of the flexible components in the use of behavioral objectives. Regardless of the competency to be achieved, each teacher has a right to be himself/herself when it comes to the art of teaching. Teachers are different. They differ in self-concepts, in ideas on teaching, subject matter competence, educational training and background, social adjustments, imagination, creativity, personality, teaching skills or abilities, and in every other respect that is subject to human change or limitation. Thus, they may be expected to utilize different methods and techniques to achieve the same competency.

Any type of appropriate activity, human and material resource, or other means may be employed. Strategies may consist of lectures, visual materials, study of printed materials, on-the-job simulations, large- and small-group interactions, or learner selection of his or her own free-choice activities from among possible alternatives. The strategies may be based upon some specific curriculum model or learning theory.

Additional Considerations of Instructional Delivery Systems

The motivation of learners is not primarily a concern of CBE, but a concern of all educational programs. It should always be considered but is not likely to be stated in an instructional module. CBE programs are, however, fortunate due to the fact that there is a close relationship between certain theoretical concepts of motivation and corresponding concepts that are associated with the behavioral objective-CBE movement.

Motivation frequently brings about student success far beyond that which would be expected according to a student's measured innate abilities and acquired skills. An illustration can be made in which graduate colleges are known to place great emphasis upon past grade point averages, the Graduate Record Exam (GRE), or other scores when considering student admission into their graduate level programs. Usually a three point average in upper division college level work and/or a GRE score of over 1,000 are necessary. Through certain programs, however, perhaps ten percent of the students can be admitted who do not meet these requirements. It is often difficult to account for the fact that many students with two point averages and GRE scores as low as seven hundred are apparently able to achieve graduate level work as successfully as those who possess the normal entrance requirements.

The answer most frequently given is motivation. Motivation is an affective condition which may exist within a student whose feelings toward a particular task, object, or variable have been positively reinforced to the point that the task has become psychologically desirable. Thus, the job of the educator is to positively reinforce each student's learning experiences in whatever ways are at his/her disposal.

Harrow[1] refers to a continuum of motivation which includes a hierarchical ordering of steps, referred to as interest, appreciation, attitude, value, and life adjustment. She states: "A student's interest must first be captured; once you have his/her attention he/she can acquire some knowledge. The greater satisfaction, in terms of success, that this knowledge/skill level brings to the student, the more appreciation for the activity he/she will develop. From this appreciation, the student begins to structure a set of attitudes toward a particular activity or concept. As the attitude becomes more positive, the student progresses through higher levels of mastery skill development from which a set of values can emerge.

It is from a well-developed set of values that changes in life style emerge . . . . To reinforce motivation, it is important to identify the prerequisite experiences necessary for new situations, thereby allowing a student to begin a new learning experience from previous learning."

There are many motivation and learning theories and much controversy concerning the merits of each. Two well-known concepts that are practical and applicable to the behavioral objective and CBE movements are Herzberg's motivation theory, based upon psychological growth in relationship to job application, and Bloom's contribution toward the mastery learning concept. Student successes can, in part, be attributed to the practical influence these theories have had on the CBE program.

Herzberg[2] states that there are five motivational factors, which include:

(1) personal knowledge of achievement;

(2) recognition of the achievement by others;

(3) the work itself;

(4) responsibility; and

(5) advancement and growth.

Each of these factors represents a potentially strong reason why the use of behavioral objectives can move the CBE programs closer to a polar extreme representing panacea. Positive reinforcement of the student by all factors could be a greater stimulus for success than any other one strategy that can be applied.

Using the University of North Florida (UNF) as an example, we find that several of these motivational factors appear in the design of competency-based education programs. The content of each course in Educational Administration consists of challenging individual and group assignments designed to produce educational leaders at the building level, as well as leaders in the use of the systems approach for comprehensive planning and problem-solving. Each student is required to achieve all competencies in the modules he/she undertakes.

Additional key characteristics of the program are continuous feedback to the students of their competency achievement and the opportunity to recycle for achievement when unsuccessful on the first attempt. The recycle opportunities help individualize a student's instruction, utilizing either the same or individually prescribed enabling strategies.

The combined total of all of the experiences the student receives provides him/her with some contact with each of the five motivational factors, although, admittedly, all students do not receive the same experience, feedback, or emphasis upon motivation by their instructors. The point is that the nature of the program itself would insure some emphasis upon at least two or three of the motivational factors.

Bloom *et al.*[3] assert that perhaps 85 to 95 percent of the students can master the learning concepts or tasks to which they are exposed. It is, therefore, the task of the teacher to determine the strategies which will enable students to master the content to which they are assigned.

The teacher's task, under this concept, is to determine the appropriate concepts or competencies to be achieved, what will be accepted as evidence of concept mastery, and the development of appropriate methods, materials, and procedures to ensure that the greatest percentage possible of the student population does attain mastery. It can be assumed that students will better enjoy or be more motivated toward instructional opportunities which provide them success than toward instructional opportunities that may be unclear or ones in which failure is imminent.

Several characteristics of CBE help ensure student achievement of the desired competencies in a manner that is supportive of the Bloom mastery learning concept. First, the recycle opportunities (included in the enabling strategies) provide the student with a second or even third chance to succeed in the event he/she is not successful the first time. The recycle technique provides the student with additional time, which is often all that is necessary for a learner to attain mastery of a learning task.

Many recycle opportunities provide students with additional individualized enabling strategies to guide their learning efforts. CBE also measures a student's achievement against completion of competencies and objectives, rather than comparing him/her to a norm or placing him/her on a curve that is designed to detect differences among learners. Norm comparisons force the failure of some students, whereas measuring student achievement against completion of objectives allows the learner to be evaluated according to what he/she knows rather than how he/she compares with others.

The ideas of Herzberg and Bloom, as well as those of other "educative experts," have been woven into the UNF program of CBE. Both program and student evaluation to date have been rewarding.

Four types of measurements have been used to provide evaluative information. These measures include (1) quarterly course evaluations, (2) exit interview evaluations from students completing the program, (3) university-wide program evaluations once a year, and (4) surveys of administrators who employ students graduating from the program. Analysis and summary of all of these evaluations to date reveal these generalizable results:

(1) high student satisfaction with the graduate program;

(2) top job performance ratings by administrators of school systems employing UNF graduates;

(3) students rate the CBE program as being superior to the traditional experience-based programs;

(4) strong encouragement of peer teachers to attend the University of North Florida by students who have graduated from UNF; and

(5) positive rating in all other program categories related to either student or program success.

Yes, CBE, designed to motivate students, can result in students achieving more, as evidenced by higher scores or better assessment performances. This has been the experience at the University of North Florida. Admittedly, this data is situation-specific and strong generalizations cannot be made at this point. It must be remembered, however, that the reason students achieve more, and, perhaps, receive higher marks, is because they *learn* more. Continuous recycling of competencies not achieved on the first attempt and alternative individualized strategies prevent students from exiting the courses without an acceptable amount of competency being achieved.

Some "behavior modification" techniques can be considered to be strong motivational factors, particularly when the learners represent students of an elementary and secondary school age. Most universities are placing a strong emphasis in this area in their teacher education programs.

Behavior modification requires the identification by the teacher of desirable classroom behaviors and, then, structuring or restructuring the environment so that undesirable behavior is eliminated and desirable behavior occurs. Students may be rewarded for positive behaviors, but receive no such reward for negative responses. There is little need at this point, nor is it our intent, to explore behavior modification or any other form of motivation in great depth. Motivation is not unique to programs based upon the use of behavioral objectives. The significant factor is that, if an instructional delivery system is to represent all strategies necessary to achieve concept mastery, then motivation must not be ignored, although it may occur outside the limits of competency modules. CBE can and does result in better delivery systems, due to visibility requirements that are placed upon them. These systems are written and, for the most part, are placed inside competency modules, with alternative strategies provided. This results in more self-motivation and in-service training on the part of the teacher. In addition, the clarity and specificity of the competency statements aid the teacher in strategy preparation and student evaluation.

Summing up instructional delivery systems, the reader should keep the following in mind:

1. Instructional delivery systems are means rather than ends.
2. It is the right of each teacher to prepare his/her own strategies for achieving competencies.
3. Alternative strategies should be provided for achieving each competency.
4. Strategies for CBE instructional delivery systems tend to be better devised and organized than was the case with traditional instructional programs.
5. Instructional delivery systems and/or strategies should be devised to achieve competencies or learning intents rather than behavioral outcomes.
6. CBE program planners should give consideration to sound learning and motivational theories that can be applied in a practical manner to aid student achievement.
7. Student motivation can be as essential to learning achievement as is student aptitude.
8. Providing students with recycling opportunities and alternative strategies is consistent with accepted concepts of both motivation and learning.
9. Students need to (a) be psychologically fulfilled by their study assignments, (b) know they can succeed, (c) be recognized for their achievement, and (d) be responsible for their own study assignments, as well as their general advancement and growth.
10. Carefully planned CBE programs provide the essential motivational and learning components necessary for student achievement.

Glossary of Key Chapter Terms

Competency Module: The basic component of an instructional delivery system, representing competency-based education. It represents a guide for students and a teaching plan for instructors.

Instructional Delivery System: All of the enabling activities, resources, and other phenomena that are developed by teachers as strategies to aid students to achieve the competencies to which they are assigned.

Notes

1. Anita J. Harrow. "The Behavioral Objectives Movement: Its Impact on Physical Education." *Educational Technology*, Vol. 17, No. 6 (June), 1977, pp. 31-38.
2. Frederick Herzberg. "One More Time: How Do You Motivate Employees?" *Harvard Business Review*, January-February, 1968, pp. 53-62.
3. B. S. Bloom, J. T. Hastings, and G. F. Madaus. *Handbook of Summative and Formative Evaluation of Student Learning* (New York: McGraw Hill, 1971).

VI.

Guidelines for Writing Competencies: Goal Statements

"That man may safely venture on his way, who is so guided that he cannot stray."

—Walter Scott

"Common sense is the knack of seeing things as they are, and doing things as they ought to be done."

—C. E. Stowe

CHAPTER GOALS
The reader should:
1. develop skill in using the goals approach writing technique to state simple cognitive competencies (goals);
2. develop the ability to apply systems processes in breaking down a unit of content into specific competency (goal) statements.

When using any guidelines, the reader should keep two things in mind. First, guidelines are models and, thus, are flexible. Secondly, most guidelines or models cannot be proved to be either right or wrong, but can be considered correct if they serve the function for which they are intended. It is with these thoughts in mind that the author has developed the "goals approach" to writing competency statements and behavioral objectives.

At least four attributes are necessary for a person to become proficient in writing competencies and their corresponding behavioral outcomes: (1) thorough conceptualization of the goal-setting and objective development processes; (2) comprehension of the writing technique; (3) subject area expertise in the content areas in which goals and objectives will be stated; and (4) the ability to structure reasonably stated sentences. It is the intent of the author to provide the reader with the necessary goal-setting and objective specification conceptualization, as well as an understanding of the "goals approach" writing technique. However, it will be necessary for the readers to supply their own subject area expertise and sentence writing ability that are essential if the competencies and objectives they write are to communicate well with their intended audiences.

The first problem of concern in the adoption of guidelines for writing competency statements is for the educator to make a decision concerning the purpose of education. Just what is teaching and learning all about? Is the purpose of our instructional efforts to, primarily, train students to perform well defined tasks or to develop more fully their total capabilities including the learning of broad areas of content and the abilities to apply intellectual operations involving various levels of understanding to that content? The "goals approach" assumes that both content mastery and the intellectual levels of application of the content into real-life situations are the real purposes of educating students.

A second problem in presenting a new objective writing technique is to determine the manner in which to present the guidelines to the learner, one step at a time or as a total entity. In other words, should the guidelines present both content mastery and the intellectual levels of applications as simultaneous learning experiences, or should content identification be presented first and, subsequently, be related to intellectual applications as a sequential process.

Years of experience in training teachers, in goal setting, and in the writing and use of performance objectives, has convinced the author that the only way for a student to properly internalize the process is to proceed sequentially, one step at a time, and to pursue each step in great depth. Thus, the guidelines of this text, representing the "goals approach" for writing performance objectives, are presented so that the reader will acquire the necessary understandings as they occur in the following logical sequential order: the development of

(1) appropriate concepts;

(2) skill in identifying basic cognitive content as competencies written as goal statements;

(3) skill in converting basic cognitive competencies into behavioral objectives; and

(4) the ability to further operationalize cognitive competency statements by adapting them to the six hierarchical levels of understanding including complex behaviors.

Steps two, three, and four are the subjects of Chapters VI, VII, and VIII of this text.

Writing Competency Statements: Learning Oriented Goals

In Chapter II, it was pointed out that one of the advantages of CBE over the experience-based programs was the better communication to the students of the learning tasks that they are expected to achieve. These learning tasks can be referred to as competencies, which are best stated as instructional goals. These competencies, hence goals, should be conceptualized by the reader as being the targets or desired ends of any instructional program.

The chief concerns of an educator in the preliminary stages of learning to write goal statements are that: (1) the content of the competency be appropriate, (2) the domain be properly identified, and (3) the total competency statement communicates well to the student and any other audience for whom it is intended. In order to achieve each of these criteria, it is essential that the goal-setting technique used to identify the competency be accurate and that each competency is carefully checked to be sure the minimum component parts necessary are clearly stated.

The Basic Goal Statement
    The basic goal statement represents a preliminary rendering of instructional intent based upon some content that has been identified as being appropriate for a learner or learner group. The teacher merely takes the content, representing a desired competency, and writes a one sentence goal statement such as the following examples:

1. Students in Home Economics 100 *will acquire an understanding of the terms "grain" and "off-grain" as they relate to fabric.*
2. Environmental studies students *will acquire an understanding of the land use categories commonly accepted and used by urban planners.*
3. Home economics students *will develop an understanding of how to distinguish between a nap fabric material and a material without fabric nap.*
4. Jane Adams *will develop an understanding of certain vocabulary words used in selected short stories.*
5. Literature Nine students *will develop an understanding of the elements of a short story.*
6. Literature Nine students *will acquire an understanding of how an original character sketch is written.*
7. Sophomore home economics students *will develop an understanding of the selection of a suitable fabric for a chosen garment.*
8. Third level primary students *will increase their understanding of terminology necessary in using an encyclopedia.*
9. Ninth grade English students *will improve their understanding of facts concerning our black American writers.*
10. Seventh grade English students *will acquire an understanding of the conventional patterns of heroic traditions found in many Greek myths.*

11. Accounting students at Ribault High School *will acquire an understanding of the fundamental elements of the accounting equation utilized as the basic criteria for determining what a business owns, owes, and is worth.*
12. The advanced crafts class *will develop an understanding of the technique necessary to draw a simple outline of a face.*

Each of these goal statements, as will be the case with all of the example goals and objectives used as illustrations in the following chapters of this text, was written by a public school teacher in his/ her first attempt to identify competencies through the use of goal statements. None of these goals were difficult for the teachers to identify by their own goal-setting process. Once stated, it is necessary for the person writing the goal statements to check them to determine if they communicate well to the intended audience.

Checking Goal Statements for Appropriate Communication

The idea of the communication check was taken from the Management By Objectives (MBO) goal-setting process, which is designed to establish the task to be accomplished and the person who will be accountable for achieving the task. The tasks identified in MBO and by the use of techniques, such as systems analysis, are primarily non-learning oriented in nature and are usually stated as goals that establish: (1) who, (2) what, and (3) when. This can be interpreted as who is responsible for what, and when the task must be completed.

The communication check of goal statements is primarily a concern of and for the benefit of the person writing the goal statements. It helps an educator focus upon the correct target of his/ her instructional activities, as well as to build his/her own confidence in goal-setting and objective-writing techniques. It assures the learner of understanding the intent of the goal on, at least, a minimum acceptable level of communication.

The communication check consists of two components: (1) the identification of the accountable learner or learner group for which the objective is being stated; and (2) the identification of a complete learning task. These two components are defined as (1) the accountable learner or learner group and (2) the learning task.

Accountable Learner or Learner Group

The learner or learner group refers to the person or persons who are to be held accountable for assuming the responsibility of achieving the competency. In other words, the learner or learner group identifies the person or persons who will be evaluated for a change in cognitive, affective, or psychomotor behavior which has resulted from the enabling activities used to attain the *learning task*, or end, dictated in the goal statement.

Learning Task

The learning task represents all of the goal statement, exclusive of the identified learner or learner group. This component consists of three parts: (1) the content, (2) the behavioral domain classification, and (3) the use of future time orientation. The content specifies that which is to be learned and later evaluated. The behavioral domain refers to the cognitive, affective, and psychomotor domains of behavior:

1. *Cognitive Domain*: Behaviors that deal with the recall of knowledge and development of intellectual skills and abilities commonly referred to as complex behaviors.
2. *Affective Domain*: Behaviors which refer to feelings and emotions or which describe changes in interests, appreciations, attitudes, values, and adjustments.
3. *Psychomotor Domain*: Behaviors which are primarily concerned with the performance of voluntary movement and perceptual-motor activities.

This chapter is primarily concerned with the development of the technique for writing goal statements. Thus, emphasis in the learning tasks will be placed upon the identification of future time orientation, content, and domain only, rather than in more fully operationalizing the goals through identification of various domain classification levels. Writing objectives by cognitive classification levels will be the purpose of Chapter VIII.

Goal Statement Critique

The person writing competencies as goal statements will be the only one, in all probability, who will ever critique a goal statement. The critique is made for the express purpose of increasing the writer's proficiency in the specification of his/her instructional intents. Six goals previously stated in this chapter will serve as examples to illustrate the mental process that is used in critiquing goal statements.

1. Students in Home Economics 100 will acquire an understanding of the terms "grain" and "off-grain" as they relate to fabric.
   Critique:
   A. Learner Group—Students in Home Economics 100
   B. Learning Task—
      (1) Content—terms "grain" and "off-grain"
      (2) Domain—Cognitive (understanding)
      (3) Future Time Orientation—will acquire
2. Environmental studies students will acquire an understanding of the land use categories commonly accepted and used by urban planners.
   Critique:
   A. Learner Group—Environmental studies students
   B. Learning Task—
      (1) Content—land use categories ... used by urban planners
      (2) Domain—Cognitive (understanding)
      (3) Future Time Orientation—will acquire
3. Home economics students will develop an understanding of how to distinguish between a nap fabric material and a material without nap fabric.
   Critique:
   A. Learner Group—Home economics students
   B. Learning Task—
      (1) Content—nap fabric material and without nap fabric material
      (2) Domain—Cognitive (understanding)
      (3) Future Time Orientation—will develop

4. Jane Adams will develop an understanding of certain vocabulary words used in selected short stories.
   Critique:
   A. Learner—Jane Adams
   B. Learning Task—
      (1) Content—vocabulary words ... short stories
      (2) Domain—Cognitive (understanding)
      (3) Future Time Orientation—will develop
5. Third level primary students will increase their understanding of terminology necessary in using an encyclopedia.
   Critique:
   A. Learner Group—Third level primary students
   B. Learning Task—
      (1) Content—terminology ... encyclopedia
      (2) Domain—Cognitive (understanding)
      (3) Future Time Orientation—will increase
6. Ninth grade English students will improve their understanding of facts concerning our black American writers.
   Critique:
   A. Learner Group—Ninth grade English students
   B. Learning Task—
      (1) Content—facts concerning black American writers
      (2) Domain—Cognitive (understanding)
      (3) Future Time Orientation—will improve

The reader will note that each of these competency (goal) statements identifies first of all the learner or learner group accountable for achieving the competency. This information should always be apparent to the teacher when competencies are being selected, particularly if his/her instructional strategies are to be individualized for use with some learners. The identification of the learner or learner group can be omitted in each competency (goal) statement that is to be used in a competency module or similar guideline which provides this information on its "heading page" or in some similar manner.

Second, the learning task in each competency can be seen to represent the cognitive domain in its broadest context, understanding; see Figure 6.1.

No further identification is needed at this point to assist the

Figure 6.1. Cognitive domain in its broadest context, understanding.

UNDERSTANDING	
	1.00 —
	2.00 —
	3.00 —
	4.00 —
	5.00 —
	6.00 —

learner in understanding what is meant by domain classification. In fact, to attempt to teach the six classification levels and sub-categories at this point can be self-defeating. Emphasis must remain upon learning the writing technique, not in operationalizing it in its final form.

Once an educator envisions who his/her learner is and the domain of interest, it is relatively simple to write the goal statement with a future time orientation for some specifically identified content. Another point to remember is that the choice of terms, such as "to understand," "to appreciate," and others, is perfectly acceptable in the development of a competency (goal) statement. They are not acceptable as indicators of behavior or performance when stated as a behavioral outcome. Again, the reader must keep in mind that the competency, goal, or learning intent is not the same thing as the behavioral outcome, and each of the two components must meet its own criteria.

Goal Setting for Competency Identification

The problem of goal setting to determine appropriate competencies has been one of the greatest hindrances to the development of adequate performance objectives. Unless an educational program attempts to achieve appropriate competencies, it won't make any difference how good the instructional strategies are or how accurately achievement is assessed; the program will still have little value. Thus, it is again evident that goal identification, rather than evaluation of performance, is the first and most important function in the development of performance objectives.

There are many goal-setting methods, each of which has its own advantages and uses. Among these goal-setting techniques are:

1. *Management By Objectives*. This is a technique employed by business and industry to establish personnel and program accountability. It begins with top management and filters down. Its use results in goals which are primarily non-learning oriented and not concerned with content. Thus, it has little value as a tool for setting competencies.

2. *Systems Analysis*. This represents a problem-solving technique that is primarily useful in activities involving comprehensive planning. It is primarily concerned with determining what functions, activities, or tasks must be accomplished in order for people to accomplish an assigned mission. The goals and objectives resulting from this approach are primarily non-learning oriented and not concerned with content. As is the case with MBO, they have little value for establishing competencies.

3. *Task Analysis*. This technique, which can be an off-shoot of the task analysis performed as the final step in systems analysis, may result in either learning oriented or non-learning oriented goals. For example, the tasks performed by a school principal can be analyzed according to the functions he/she performs. They can then be stated as goals which would represent competencies needed to be

achieved by future educational administrators. This technique can be applied to various instructional areas, but it is not the best method for determining content and requires much time and preparation to perform adequately.

4. *Needs Assessment.* This method can be used in establishing either learning oriented or non-learning oriented goals. Usually a needs assessment will result in determining areas in which discrepancies are identified based upon the difference between a present condition and a desired condition. Goals can be established, which, if achieved, will eliminate the discrepancies for which they have been stated.

5. *Theoretical, Professional Judgment, and Textbook Approaches.* These three approaches can also be used to identify either learning oriented or non-learning oriented goals, but each has very limited application for the educational scene and will not be pursued in depth in this text.

6. *Systematic Competency Analysis. This is probably the most useful of all of the approaches to the identification of content and one that is very easy to learn and apply. It is this concept that we will present and recommend for greatest use in competency identification.*

Systematic Competency Analysis

Systematic competency analysis is an adaptation of the systems analysis process for the purpose of determining content rather than functions or activities. It begins with some broad area of content, which can be referred to as the content mission. The content area is then broken down into smaller and more specific content areas, referred to as subsystems. This is accomplished by answering the question: What are the major areas of content included within the content mission? As soon as the content subsystems are identified they are broken down further into subsystem components and, then, interim components as needed. This is accomplished by answering the question: What are the smaller and more specific areas of content included within the subsystem or subsystem component? Each content subsystem is broken down in this manner until the identified content reaches the level of specificity at which the teacher wishes to convert it into a competency or goal statement.

The use of the systematic competency analysis technique is equivalent to the determination of specifics from various levels of abstraction through a process of division. There is no limit to the number of levels of breakdown which may be performed and no requirement for any minimum number of levels which must be broken down.

Identifying the content mission is the first phase of goal setting. The mission goal will establish the overall content intent of the program being developed. A goal stated at this level will be broad or general in scope and will globally define the content system to be developed. For purposes of illustration, Barger[1] developed a system for the area of general math. A mission goal might be stated for this system as follows: Ninth grade math students will acquire an understanding of General Math.

The content mission goal will represent the broadest goal for the content systems and will need to be broken into subsystems. This breakdown of the mission goal can be shown as demonstrated in Figure 6.2.

As soon as the subsystems are identified, the teacher must make a decision as to whether the content has or has not reached the necessary level of specificity for conversion to competency statements. Assuming this is not yet the case and that it will require further breakdown to at least the level of interim components, the teacher will proceed to break each subsystem down into subsystem components and, then, into interim components, as shown in Figure 6.3.

At this level of specificity, the teacher will write his/her basic goal statements that will later become the basis for his/her operationalized behavioral objectives, as outlined in Chapter VIII of this

Figure 6.2. Breakdown of mission goal.

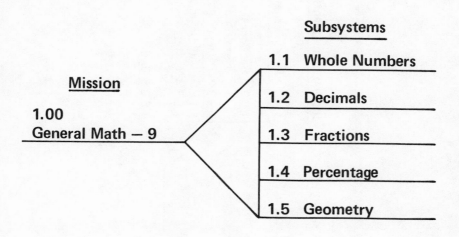

text. Goal statements for the interim components identified in the General Math system were stated as shown in Figure 6.3.

1.5.3.1   Ninth grade general math students will acquire an understanding of the formula for area of a parallelogram, a=bh.

1.5.3.2   Ninth grade general math students will acquire an understanding of the formula for area of a rectangle, a=lw.

1.5.3.3   Ninth grade general math students will acquire an understanding of the formula for area of a triangle, a=½bh.

1.5.3.4   Ninth grade general math students will acquire an understanding of the formula for area of a trapezoid, a=½h (a+b).

1.5.3.5   Ninth grade general math students will acquire an understanding of the formula for area of a circle, a=πr^2.

Osborne[2] used the systematic competency analysis technique, under a different format, to identify basic goal statements for a

Figure 6.3. Breakdown of one subsystem into subsystem components and interim components.

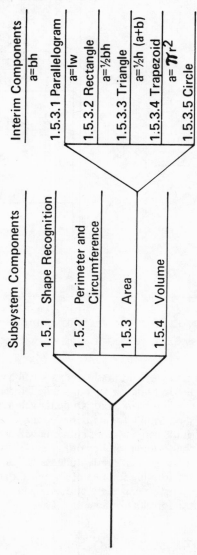

course in United States History. Her system is graphically illustrated in Figure 6.4.

This system resulted in the following goal statements being stated at the interim component level:

1.4.3.1 Eleventh grade United States History students will acquire an understanding of Alexander Hamilton's philosophy of government.

1.4.3.2 Eleventh grade United States History students will acquire an understanding of Thomas Jefferson's philosophy of government.

1.4.3.3 Eleventh grade United States History students will acquire an understanding of the development of the Federalist Party into the Republican Party.

1.4.3.4 Eleventh grade United States History students will acquire an understanding of the development of the Democratic-Republican Party into the Democratic Party.

It is important to remember that the teacher has full control of the level at which the competencies are stated as goal statements. In some instances, a breakdown to the level of subsystem components will be sufficient. At other times, the breakdown may exceed the level of interim components. This depends upon the content areas involved and the level of abstraction at which the mission is identified at the system level.

A simple systems coding technique is employed to identify the levels of systematic competency analysis as well as to identify each of the systems component competencies. The key to the coding is as follows:

System — identified by the first digit on the left of the first decimal, e.g., 1.00.

Subsystem — identified by the digit(s) to the right of the first decimal, e.g., 1.4 (subsystems are arranged sequentially; the number of the digit indicates the serial position of the subsystem); e.g., 1.4 indicates it is the fourth subsystem in system number 1.

Figure 6.4. Use of systematic competency analysis techniques to identify goals in United States History.

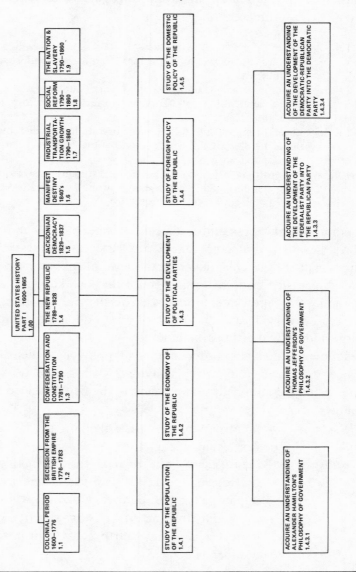

Subsystem

Component —identified by the digit(s) to the right of the second decimal, e.g., 1.4.3 (subsystem components are arranged sequentially; therefore, the number of the digit indicates the serial position of the subsystem component); e.g., 1.4.3 indicates it is the third subsystem component in the fourth subsystem in system number 1.

Interim

Component —identified by the digit(s) to the right of the third decimal, e.g., 1.4.3.10 indicates it is the tenth interim component within the third subsystem component belonging to the fourth subsystem in system number 1. Systems may be broken down into an unlimited number of levels. Another decimal and number are added for each additional level that is broken down, and these can be referred to as interim component levels two, three, four, etc.

The following illustration, representing a system broken down into seven levels, may clarify the above explanation of coding:

Identifies system		Identifies subsystem		Identifies subsystem component		Identifies interim component		Identifies level two interim component		Identifies level three interim component		Identifies level four interim component
1	•	4	•	3	•	10	•	3	•	6	•	2

The reader should note that coding in this fashion allows for an infinite number of subsystem, subsystem components, and interim components. This assures the curriculum planner of being able to attain the desired level of content specificity, regardless of how abstractly the content mission has been identified at the system level.

Summary

This chapter has presented a technique for developing skills in using the "goals approach" writing technique to state simple cognitive competencies. First, the writing concept is developed along with a technique for checking basic goal statements to insure that they communicate adequately the content of the competency.

Second, these preliminary basic goal statements are written to establish the term *understanding* as representing a broad area referred to as the cognitive domain. No attempt is made at this point to further operationalize the goal statements to specify levels of cognitive understanding.

Finally, several goal-setting techniques were reviewed. One of these, systematic competency analysis, was chosen as a process that can be effectively used to analyze a content area or course into all of its identifiable essential content components. The next chapter, Chapter VII, will reveal how these simple competency statements can be used to develop an understanding of the concept of the "goals approach" to writing behavioral objectives. Chapter VIII will then build upon the foundation presented in Chapters VI and VII to include the operationalization of the behavioral objective-writing technique through the use of the classification levels and sub-categories of the cognitive taxonomy.

Notes

1. C. A. Barger, Junior High Math Teacher, Ribault Junior High School, Duval County School System, Jacksonville, Florida.
2. Brenda C. Osborne, Assistant Principal, Orange Park High School, Clay County School System, Orange Park, Florida.

VII.

Writing Behavioral Outcomes: Converting Goals to Objectives

"Think wrongly, if you please; but in all cases think for yourself."
—Lessing

"Judge a man by his questions rather than by his answers."
—Voltaire

CHAPTER GOALS

The reader should:

1. acquire comprehension of the technique for writing behavioral objectives by the "goals approach";
2. develop skill in using the "goals approach" writing technique to state basic cognitive behavioral objectives.

In Chapter IV, behavioral outcomes were revealed to be responses that a learner can exhibit as evidence that he/she has achieved a desired competency or has learned something. Within this context, a behavioral outcome becomes an evaluation or assessment mode. Evaluation is the process, formal and informal, of providing information for decision-makers. It usually involves: (1) setting goals; (2) specifying objectives; (3) collecting data through various measurement activities; (4) analyzing the data; and (5) decision-making.

Behavioral outcomes represent the evaluation component concerned with data collection through some performance, behavioral activity, or instrumentation chosen as a means of estimating student learning achievements. These behavioral outcomes involve: (1) oral response; (2) written response; and (3) demonstration types of responses which may or may not include oral or written behaviors.

Primary Concerns of Measurement: Behavioral Outcomes

In choosing a behavioral outcome, the person writing an objective should keep in mind that any outcome performance selected represents only one of many alternative behaviors which could be selected as representing a means for determining success in achieving the competency for which it has been selected. Thus, it is important that an effort be made to select some behavioral activity that can be said to truly represent a response that the learner would likely be able to make as a result of learning achievement.

Four concerns of an objective developer should be the:

(1) congruency between the original competency and the behavioral outcome chosen to represent successful competency achievement. In other words, the identification of the correct type of performance, behavioral activity, or instrumentation;

(2) identification of appropriate situations in which to observe the measurable performances under normal circumstances;

(3) determination of the proper criteria to be used in establishing the minimum standard or level of success that is necessary; and

(4) collection of all of the desired data concerning the behaviors exhibited without contaminating the evaluation evidence that each behavior represents.

Criterion-Referenced Behavioral Objectives

According to the "goals approach" objective-writing technique, all performance or behavioral objectives should have two distinct characteristics: *goal* and *evaluation statements*. These represent statements of the competency or learning outcome to be achieved and the behavioral outcome that represents how success in achieving the competency will be determined.

Writing goal statements was the topic of Chapter VI. Converting goals to behavioral objectives requires the addition of a basic statement of a behavioral performance that will be acceptable as a measure of success plus the inclusion of a success level criterion standard. The completed behavioral objective statement can then be referred to as a *criterion-referenced behavioral objective*. It consists of a goal, which is the competency, purpose, or desired end that is sought; a measurable behavioral performance; and criteria for determining the minimum level at which the behavioral activity will be considered acceptable.

Figure 7.1 illustrates the requirements of a criterion-referenced behavioral objective. Obviously, as the name implies, it is not essential that any objective have an optional statement as is shown in Figure 7.1 It is included in the objective illustration as a reminder that sometimes the behavioral outcome statements may need some assistance in communicating their full meaning to the target audience. In Chapter VI, twelve goal statements were listed and six of them critiqued. Behavioral objectives can be developed from these goals as follows:

1. Students in Home Economics 100 will acquire an understanding of the terms "grain" and "off-grain" as they relate to fabric. Success will be determined by their writing, without error, the definition of the two terms and illustration of each with a simple drawing.

Figure 7.1. Requirements of a criterion-referenced behavioral objective.

LEARNING
ORIENTED
(BEHAVIORAL)
OBJECTIVES

A.   GOAL (Competency Statement)

Basic statement of intent with communication checks:
1. Accountable learner or learner group
2. Learning task:

  a. content
  b. behavioral domain classification
  c. use of future time orientation

B.   EVALUATION (Behavioral Outcome)

Basic statement of how successful competency achievement
will be determined.
1. Performance: behavioral activity or instrumentation
2. Success level criterion standard

C.   OPTIONAL STATEMENTS

   Additional information such as givens, conditions, or
teacher expectancies for proportional student achievement.
These statements can aid in communicating an objective's
evaluation requirement to the student audience for which
the objective is intended.

2. Environmental studies students will acquire an understanding of the land use categories commonly accepted and used by urban planners, so that when given a written 20-item short answer test that presents descriptions of urban land uses, students will be able to correctly name the proper category designation for at least 75% of the items.

3. Home economics students will develop an understanding of how to distinguish between a nap fabric and a fabric without nap, so that when given ten fabric swatches to be identified through either visual or tactile discrimination, the students will orally identify at least nine correctly.

4. Jane Adams will develop an understanding of certain vocabulary words used in selected short stories, so that when given a list of 20 vocabulary words taken from several short stories read in or out of class, and their definitions, she will use at least 17 of the words correctly in an original written sentence according to the judgment of the teacher.

5. Literature Nine students will develop an understanding of the elements of a short story, so that when given an unfamiliar short story to read and two particular elements of the short story (i.e., character, plot, setting, theme, point of view), they will prepare a written analysis in a minimum of one paragraph. The teacher's judgment will serve as the standard for determining success.

6. Literature Nine students will acquire an understanding of how to write an original character sketch. Success in achieving this goal will be evidenced by a written two-three page description of a person of their own choosing that correctly includes, according to their teacher's judgment, the following criteria:

1. A physical description of the person.
2. The character's background or personal history.
3. The character's surroundings, such as his/her room or office.
4. The character's thoughts, emotions, and values.
5. The character's actions and reactions and opinions of others.
6. The character's speech.
7. The opinions or reactions of others to what the character does or says.

7. Sophomore home economics students will develop an understanding of how to select suitable fabric for a chosen garment, so that when given the opportunity to orally select a woven fabric for a garment of their choice, it will, according to the teacher's judgment, correctly meet the following criteria:

1. If a designed fabric is selected, it must be an all-over design.
2. The fabric selected must be without nap.
3. The fabric must create the illusion they are trying to achieve.
4. The fabric should be "grain" perfect or, if it is "off-grain," this should not be more than one and one-half inches.

8. Third level primary students will increase their understanding of ter-

minology that is helpful in using an encyclopedia, so that when asked to write definitions of five terms commonly used in using an encyclopedia, 75% of the students will be able to do so with 90% accuracy.

9. Ninth grade English students will improve their understanding of facts concerning black American writers, so that when given written lists of 20 black writers and the titles of 20 works of poetry, short stories, etc., 90% of the students will be able to orally match the writers to their own works with 100% accuracy.

10. Seventh grade English students will acquire an understanding of the conventional patterns of heroic traditions found in many Greek myths, so that when given a list of ten characteristics of literature—five miscellaneous and five taken from mythology—the students will correctly identify the five characteristics which were used in the traditional heroic myths of the Greek storytellers.

11. Accounting students at Ribault High School will acquire an understanding of the fundamental elements of the accounting equation utilized as the basic criteria for determining what a business owns, owes, and is worth. Success in achieving this goal will be evidenced by the students listing and defining in writing each of the three elements with 100% accuracy.

12. The advanced crafts class will develop an understanding of the technique necessary to draw a simple outline of a face, so that when required to give an oral description of how to draw a face, the students will give each of the four steps in the correct chronological order.

Since these objectives were chosen primarily for the purpose of illustrating the "goals approach" writing technique, a question can immediately be raised concerning the wording chosen for indicating future time orientation in objectives eight and nine. The words "will increase" and "will improve" both imply that a beginning point is known or has been determined. This being the case, to increase or improve means to make a gain from a previously identified observation to another later observation of the same nature to determine if change has occurred.

One indicator of a behavioral outcome's congruency with the goal it evaluates must, in these two instances, be the use of a before-and-after approach in the evaluation design of each of the two behavior outcomes. In other words, there would be a pre-test to determine a beginning point and a post-test to indicate gain from that beginning point. This was not the case in the evaluation components of either objective numbers eight or nine. This, of course, decreases the value of the overall objective to some extent regardless of other factors. This type of error and others may be reduced or eliminated by the objective writer mentally critiquing each of his/her objectives thoroughly prior to using them with his/her student groups.

Behavioral Outcome Critique

As indicated in the preceding chapter, the only one expected to actually critique an objective is the person who is writing it. The critique is used as a self-checking device to increase the writer's proficiency in communicating his/her intents to the target audience—the students who will attempt to achieve the objectives. The behavioral outcomes from six of the objectives previously stated in this chapter can serve well as examples to illustrate the critiquing technique for evaluation components of behavioral objectives.

1. Jane Adams will develop an understanding of certain vocabulary words used in selected short stories, *so that when given a list of 20 vocabulary words taken from several short stories read in or out of class, and their definitions, she will use at least 17 of the words correctly in an original written sentence according to the judgment of the teacher.*
   Behavioral Outcome Critique:
   A. Performance—writing an original sentence
   B. Criterion Standard—correctly using at least 17 of 20 vocabulary words
   C. Optional Statement—given a list of 20 vocabulary words ... and their definitions

2. Literature Nine students will develop an understanding of the elements of a short story, *so that when given an unfamiliar short story to read and two particular elements of the short story (i.e., character, plot, setting, theme, point of view), they will correctly prepare a written analysis in a minimum of one paragraph. The teacher's judgment will serve as the standard for determining success.*
   Behavioral Outcome Critique:
   A. Performance—preparing a written analysis
   B. Criterion Standard—the use of the teacher's judgment to determine the adequacy of the written paragraph

C. Optional Statement—given an unfamiliar short story to read and two particular elements of the short story

Note: Teacher judgment is often the determining factor in whether a student achieves success in competency achievement. However, his/her expertise is based upon his/her understanding of the requirements of an objective well enough to evaluate it according to some internal or external criteria believed to be appropriate. It is better to state the specific criteria to be used, whenever possible, rather than just to indicate teacher judgment.

3. Literature Nine students will acquire an understanding of how to write an original character sketch. *Success in achieving this goal will be evidenced by a written two-three page description of a person of their own choosing that correctly includes, according to their teacher's judgment, the following criteria:*
    1. *A physical description of the person.*
    2. *The character's background or personal history.*
    3. *The character's surroundings, such as his/her room or office.*
    4. *The character's thoughts, emotions, and values.*
    5. *The character's actions and reactions and opinions of others.*
    6. *The character's speech.*
    7. *The opinions or reactions of others to what the character does or says.*
  Behavioral Outcome Critique:
    A. Performance—a written two to three page description of a person
    B. Criterion Standard—teacher's judgment including the seven criteria statements
    C. Optional Statement—none

Note: The writer of this objective did not rely on just the identification of the teacher's judgment as the criterion for success. The seven specific criteria listed communicated the success standard much more clearly.

4. Sophomore home economics students will develop an understanding of how to select suitable fabric for a chosen garment, so *that when given the opportunity to orally select a woven fabric for a gar-*

ment of their choice, it will, according to the teacher's judgment,
correctly meet the following criteria:
  1. *If a designed fabric is selected, it must be an all-over design.*
  2. *The fabric selected must be without nap.*
  3. *The fabric must create the illusion they are trying to achieve.*
  4. *The fabric should be "grain" perfect or, if it is "off-grain," this*
     should not be more than one and one-half inches.
Behavioral Outcome Critique:
  A. Performance—orally selecting a woven fabric for a garment
  B. Criterion Standard—teacher's judgment including the four spe-
     cifically stated criteria
  C. Optional Statement—none

Note: Not all givens can be considered to be optional statements. Only the ones which can be removed without affecting the
performance or criterion standard (after some rewording) fit the
optional category. In this instance, the given was so closely related
to the requirement of the performance that it can be considered
as being necessary to the performance statement.

  5. Third level primary students will increase their understanding of
     terminology that is helpful in using an encyclopedia, *so that when*
     asked to write definitions of five terms commonly used in using an
     encyclopedia, 75% of the students will be able to do so with 90%
     accuracy.
Behavioral Outcome Critique:
  A. Performance—writing definitions of terms
  B. Criterion Standard—90% accuracy
  C. Optional Statement—75% of the students

Note: 75% of the students represents a *teacher expectancy* of
the proportion of students which he/she sets as a minimum level
goal, based upon the teacher's understanding of the realities of his/
her own student-teaching situation. It is not essential to either the
student performance or the criterion standard, which represents
the minimum student performance requirement that will be
acceptable.

Another discrepancy, in addition to the one involving the failure to make the behavioral outcome congruent with the word in-

crease in the goal statement, is that the teacher did not choose his/her student requirement (90%) carefully. Based upon the fact there are only five terms to define, the criterion standard requirement would need to be either adjusted down to 80% or adjusted upward to 100%, since it would be impossible to achieve exactly 90%. Since the goal in this objective indicates that there should have been a pre- as well as a post-test, the choice of 80% or 100% will likely depend upon the level achieved on the pre-test.

6. Ninth grade English students will improve their understanding of facts concerning black American writers, *so that when given written lists of 20 black writers and the titles of 20 works of poetry, short stories, etc., 90% of the students will be able to orally match the writers to their own works with 100% accuracy.*
Behavioral Outcome Critique:
   A. Performance—orally matching writers to their own works
   B. Criterion Standard—100% accuracy
   C. Optional Statement—given lists of 20 black writers and the titles of 20 works of poetry, short stories, etc. (In addition, "90% of the students" represents the teacher expectancy which is not a behavioral outcome requirement.)

Note: Again we can point out the fact that the evaluation component is not congruent with the words "will improve" in the goal statement. Again we emphasize that the word "improve" in the goal statement indicates there should have been a pre-test upon which the students scored less than 100% accuracy so that the achievement of all correct answers in the post-test would represent improvement. This evaluation component could have been stated as follows:

as evidenced by the students' ability to orally match 20 writers to their own works with 100% accuracy.

In this evaluation statement, both of the optional statements were omitted without changing either the performance or criterion standard.

In this chapter, we have converted goal statements into behavioral objectives by the addition of behavioral outcome statements and again illustrated a mental critiquing exercise that a writer of behavioral objectives can employ as an aid in insuring the quality of his/her behavioral objectives. It should be noted that a performance and criterion standard should be found in the evaluation component of all behavioral objectives. Optional statements are used only if they communicate information that is useful in better interpreting the requirements of the behavioral outcomes.

In each behavioral outcome statement, the important thing is that it should clearly communicate how successful attainment of the competency (goal) will be evaluated. "Goals approach" objectives are found to be a little longer than ones written by the "outcomes approach." They should be, since they communicate the purpose of each objective in addition to the behavioral outcome statement that will be used to evaluate success. The "outcomes approach" objective statements do not require the statement of purpose. Chapter VIII will be devoted to the further operationalization of behavioral objective statements.

Objectives for Use as a Practice Critiquing Exercise

The objectives that follow represent the first efforts of some teachers, representing various content areas, to write behavioral objectives by the "goals approach" writing technique. They have been stated here so that the reader may practice the objective critiquing technique outlined in Chapters VI and VII.

1. Seventh grade geography students will develop an understanding of the terminology used in identifying landforms, so that when given the names of ten landforms and 20 definitions, the students will correctly match the definitions with the landforms with 80% accuracy.

2. The specific learning disability students will acquire an understanding of the terminology that identifies the outer parts of a frog, so that when given a drawing of a frog, the students will be able to label in writing five outer parts of the frog correctly.

3. Football linemen will acquire an understanding of the terminology asso-

ciated with line play, so that when given two lists, one a list of 20 terms and the second, related duties, each lineman will successfully match 80% of the terms with their related duties.

4. The music history students will develop an understanding of the "ABA Form" of music composition. Success will be determined by the students being able to correctly label the A, B, and A sections in three of five pieces of music selected by the instructor.

5. Library aides will acquire an understanding of the circulation procedure established by the librarian for non-reference books. Success will be determined by each aide being able to explain the procedure orally, without error, or omissions.

6. Tenth grade anatomy students will develop an understanding of the circulatory system of the human body, so that when given a photo of the arteries and veins, each student will be able to correctly explain, without error, the routes in which blood leaves and returns to the heart.

7. Automotive mechanics students will develop an understanding of problems encountered in the electronic and standard battery ignition systems. Proof will be determined by 90% of the class correctly identifying eight out of ten ignition problems and correctly classifying them with the proper ignition system on a matching and essay type test.

8. Second year building trades students will acquire an understanding of how to apply the Pythagorean Theorem to squaring a building foundation so that when given the dimensions of a foundation, a 100-foot steel tape, and a table of squares and square roots, 75% of the students will lay out a foundation 11° from square, as measured by the instructor using a transit.

9. The automotive mechanics students will acquire an understanding of the use of the correct procedures to convert an engine-driven fuel pump system from a direct mechanical driven fuel system to an electrically driven fuel system and vice versa. Proof will be by 90% of the class demonstrating the procedures 100% correctly on an actual engine, as determined by the subjective judgment of the teacher.

10. Eighth grade English students will develop an understanding of the short story, so that when given the short story "The Pit and the Pendulum," by Edgar Allan Poe, students will be able to identify in writing the characters, conflict, climax, plot, protagonist, conclusion, point of view, and setting with 80% accuracy.

11. Eleventh and twelfth grade Business Law students will develop an understanding of agreements, so that when presented with five agreements, each lacking one of the five elements required for a contract, the students will be able to identify in writing the lacking element and provide in writing the correct explanation supporting each answer for at least four of the five agreements presented.

12. Distributive education students will develop an understanding of career

advancement opportunities in the field of retailing, so that when given a list of the ten job descriptions, 75% of the students will correctly be able to critique the advancement opportunities of at least 80% of the jobs on a written evaluation, according to teacher judgment.

13. Chemistry students will acquire an understanding of the products and reactants of a chemical equation, so that when given a chemical reaction, the students will identify in writing the correct products and reactants in the equation with 100% accuracy.

14. Tenth grade health students will develop an understanding of how to analyze body burns, so that when presented with five diagrams showing various body burns, 80% of the students will analyze three burns and will correctly classify each of the burns as first, second, or third degree.

15. Senior high school logic students will acquire an understanding of the relationships of the steps necessary in the problem-solving process, so that when given a list of 12 steps, the students will be able to choose without error the six correct steps in proper sequence and state in writing their relationship to problem-solving.

16. Junior college advertising students will develop an understanding of how to create unique advertising designs for a newspaper, so that when given specific criteria to follow, the students will successfully complete a design with 100% accuracy as evaluated by teacher expertise.

17. Twelfth grade Americanism versus Communism students will develop an understanding of democracy and Communism, so that when given the essay question, "Is democracy or Communism best for the United States?" the students will select either democracy or Communism and give logical reasons why the one that they selected is the best political system for the United States. Success will be determined by the subjective opinion of the instructor based on the strength of the students' argumentation.

18. Twelfth grade ecology students will develop an understanding of current world biogenic-physical problems, so that when given a one-page problem statement on oil spills containing six possible solutions and ten statements from which to select, the students will orally choose, without error, the three correct solutions, and the three correct statements which support the validity of conclusions selected.

19. College library science majors will acquire an understanding of material center programs, so that when given ten criteria for evaluation and copies of four different programs, 85% of the students will be able to select the program that best meets the criteria.

20. Senior agricultural students will acquire an understanding of cattle market conditions, so that when provided with six recent articles on cattle futures and four possible sale dates, 80% of the students will select the sale which will provide the greatest margin of profit to the cattle owner, and orally support this conclusion.

21. Design 205 students will acquire an understanding of various available heating and air conditioning systems, so that when given a proposed apartment complex plan, the students will be able to analyze the available equipment, correctly select the most practical unit, and specify it in writing. The acceptability of the choice will be determined by the opinion of the instructor.

VIII.

Operationalizing Behavioral Objectives with the Cognitive Taxonomy

"To know by rote is not knowledge; it is only a retention of what is entrusted to memory."

—Montaigne

"The essence of knowledge is, having it, to apply it; not having it...."

—Confucius

CHAPTER GOALS

The reader should:

1. develop comprehension of the values to be found in using Bloom's[1] *Taxonomy of Educational Objectives: Cognitive Domain**, to help teachers become orchestrators of the learning experiences they provide for their students;

---

*From *TAXONOMY OF EDUCATIONAL OBJECTIVES: THE CLASSIFICATION OF EDUCATIONAL GOALS: HANDBOOK 1: COGNITIVE DOMAIN*, by Benjamin S. Bloom *et al.* Copyright © 1956 by Longman, Inc. Reprinted by permission of Longman.

2. develop comprehension of the classification levels and corresponding sub-categories of both the knowledge and complex behavior levels of the cognitive taxonomy;
3. develop skill in writing behavioral objectives at the knowledge classification level of the cognitive taxonomy;
4. develop the ability to write behavioral objectives at the
   skill and ability or complex behavior classification levels of
   the cognitive taxonomy.

Chapters VI and VII have provided the reader with an understanding of the components which are essential in the "goals approach" objective-writing technique. These components consist of
a basic goal statement identifying the desired competency and a
behavioral outcome specifying how success will be evaluated in
determining competency achievement.

Both the goals and their evaluation components, identified in
Chapters VI and VII, are considered to be preliminary statements
designed primarily as an aid in helping students learn the "goals
approach" objective-writing technique. The purpose of Chapter
VIII is to assist the reader in operationalizing his/her behavioral objectives in a manner that will provide more meaningful direction
for student learning activities.

The cognitive taxonomy divides the cognitive domain into six
classification levels and 20 sub-categories of understanding and behavior that range from simple to complex. This taxonomy is written in two parts. First, the concept of understanding at the knowledge level is presented. This includes the simplest types of cognitive behaviors, involving the memory and recall type of information. This classification level includes nine sub-categories of understanding whose relationships within the knowledge level go from
the memory and recall of concrete information to the memory
and recall of more abstract data.

The second part of the taxonomy is concerned with understandings, involving the more complex behaviors. These behaviors, usually referred to as skills and abilities, are portrayed at five different classification levels, which involve 11 sub-categories. All of the classification levels are arranged in hierarchical order. In other words, they are arranged in successive order, so that each classification level and its sub-categories are thought to include and be dependent upon the one preceding it. This can be seen by reference to Figure 8.1.

The basic idea of using the taxonomy is quite simple. Knowledge, classification level 1.00, has traditionally been the most common educational goal, referring to a person being able to remember or recall something. It is considered to be basic to all other purposes of education and is the foundation for being able to understand the more complex behaviors, including the ones associated with the affective and psychomotor domains. Since knowledge is the simplest cognitive behavior, it is placed at the first level in the taxonomy.

Levels 2.00 through 6.00 refer to skills and abilities which represent complex behaviors, since they require not only knowledge, but also additional experience that can be utilized to solve new problems in new situations. Sequentially speaking, one first acquires knowledge, then develops skills and then, with appropriate combinations of knowledge and skills, one acquires abilities. Distinguishing between skills and abilities makes their use in the classification of objectives very difficult, due to the teacher not being aware of all the experiences his/her students have had in the past. For this reason, the authors of the taxonomy permit skills and abilities to be used synonymously.

Once a teacher attains mastery of the taxonomic classification levels and sub-categories, he/she can become an orchestrator of a student's learning experiences, rather than just an ordinary classroom manager. All teachers have a given number of students, along with certain materials, equipment, and a time and place for instruction. Learning is, at least, partially determined by how well

Figure 8.1. Classification levels and sub-categories of the cognitive domain.

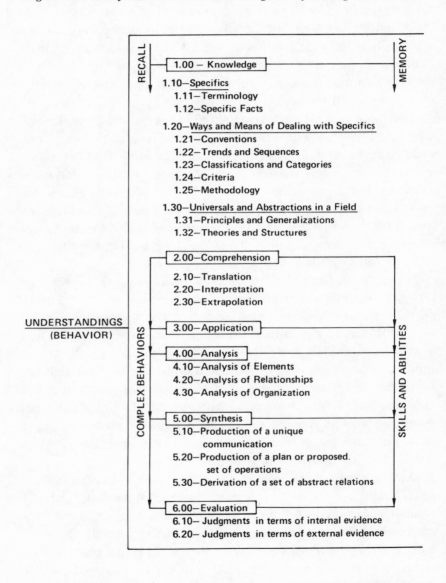

the teacher arranges or combines all of these variables, so that they will achieve the maximum effect upon the learner. Without the use of some guidelines such as offered by the taxonomy, teachers generally offer students only limited learning experiences. Effective use of the cognitive taxonomy provides teachers with the direction needed to offer students many more combinations of learning experiences, which will better insure that students develop understandings at all cognitive levels, and that they become able to perform the corresponding behaviors associated with each level of understanding.

Teachers who utilize the cognitive taxonomy find that it helps them to individualize their instruction through diagnostic teaching. They are better able to give students planned experiences at different levels of understanding. With reference to the use of objectives, the teacher is able to individualize student learning by changing: (1) the cognitive levels of understanding and behaviors; (2) the learner's criterion standard; and (3) combinations of both changes involving different goals and assessment behaviors on the part of individual students.

The major problem encountered in using the taxonomy for classification purposes is that of legitimately classifying objectives at the complex behavior levels. This is because each higher level of understanding and its corresponding behaviors require the learner to be able to understand at each of the lower levels. Thus, comprehension, application, analysis, synthesis, and evaluation are not nearly as distinct as they appear in graphic or written form.

Some objectives will be difficult to identify within one distinct classification level or one distinct sub-category, since they will appear to overlap one or more categories. Occasionally, a mistake in classification may occur, but this does not pose any threat to the value of the taxonomy.

There is no intrinsic learning value in placing any one particular objective into one of the taxonomic classification levels or into another. It is the learning that takes place that is important. The use of the taxonomy will insure that in the long run, students will achieve understandings at all six classification levels. A general rule of thumb for classifying objectives is to refer to the classification level or sub-category of a behavioral objective according to its highest level of use.

1.00—Knowledge

Objectives based upon the achievement of knowledge involve the student being able to memorize a communication and to recall it in orderly fashion when necessary. Sometimes understanding or "knowing" in this sense is referred to as rote memory. Information of this type involves the ability to memorize and the ability to bring into mind appropriate materials or information regarding specifics, ways and means of dealing with specifics, and universals and abstractions in a field.

Utilizing the objective-writing approach established in Chapters VI and VII, we can further operationalize the writing of behavioral objectives by using the taxonomy classification levels as outlined in Figure 8.1. This can be accomplished within the framework of the communication check components previously established. Each objective will still have: (1) a learner or learner group; (2) future time orientation; (3) domain identification; and (4) content in the competency or goal statement. In addition, there will be a performance and criterion in the evaluation component.

The changes to be found or differences that will occur due to the utilization of the cognitive taxonomy involve the refinement of domain identification to refer to a specific classification level of understanding in the goal accompanied by a corresponding change in how success will be evaluated, so that the behavioral outcome will be congruent with the intent of the goal. No longer will the term understanding alone be sufficient to represent the domain identification and no longer will just any behavioral outcome be acceptable to represent the requirement of student performance.

The author believes it is important for teachers to write behavioral objectives at all taxonomic classification levels. It is perhaps less important that objectives be written for each sub-category of the classification levels. The content area being studied and other variables make it unlikely that any teacher will relate his/her course of study to each of the 20 sub-categories. The purpose of emphasizing the sub-categories is that the more someone understands the component parts of a whole, the more he/she will understand the whole. It is upon this basis that the objective illustrations in this chapter have been chosen from the competency modules of various teachers representing Northeast Florida school systems.

1.10—Specifics
1.11—Terminology
You will acquire a knowledge of the terms used to identify various components of the circulatory system. Success in achieving this competency will be evidenced by your ability to correctly match at *least ten* of 15 terms with their definitions on a matching typewritten quiz.
Critique:
  I. Goal
    A. Learner—You (In competency modules the learner or learner group is usually identified on the heading page. If so, the word *you* may be substituted for the learner to indicate that this goal is for the reader, thus user, of the module.)
    B. Learning Task—
       (1) Content—terms of the circulatory system
       (2) Domain—Cognitive at 1.11 level (knowledge of the terms)
       (3) Future Time Orientation—will acquire
  II. Behavioral Outcome (Evaluation)
    A. Performance—matching terms with definitions on a written quiz
    B. Criterion Standard—match at least ten of 15 terms correctly

The important characteristic of each of the objectives written at the knowledge classification level is that the goal statements include the word knowledge and that the behavioral outcomes be stated so that the student performance requirement involves only the type of information that can be recalled from memory. The domain identification part of the goal statement for the above objective, sub-category level 1.11, could have been stated differently, as follows: (1) you will acquire an understanding at the knowledge level; or (2) you will become knowledgeable of. The rest of the objective could remain the same.

In either instance, the words "understanding at the knowledge level" or "knowledgeable" refer to the knowledge classification level, 1.00, and the word "terms" places it at the 1.11 sub-category level, knowledge of terminology. Since the definitions of terms can be memorized, it appears that being able to correctly match terms with their definitions fulfills the requirement of the behavioral outcome being congruent with the intent of the goal statement.

The relationships of the sub-categories within the knowledge level go from the knowledge of things that are concrete to the knowledge of things that are abstract. This does not alter the fact that *knowledge by any other name is still knowledge just the same*. Thus, the behavioral outcome chosen as a means of determining success must still remain as an indicator of memory recall, not the use of memory recall to show some higher level of performance. For this reason, the evaluation components of the rest of the knowledge level objectives used for illustration purposes in this chapter will not be critiqued individually. In each instance, their only specific requirements are to include behavioral performances and appropriate criteria which can represent a student's ability to recall information from memory.

1.12—Specific Facts
    You will acquire knowledge of the services performed for customers by a bank. Success will be determined by your ability to identify and place the correct service performed into the space matching a description of the service in at least 15 of the 20 items given on a written exam.
    Critique:
        I. Goal
            A. Learner—You
            B. Learning Task—
                (1) Content—services performed for customers by a bank

(2) Domain—Cognitive at 1.12 level (knowledge of services)

(3) Future Time Orientation—will acquire

II. Behavioral Outcome (Evaluation)

Performance and criterion are congruent with the knowledge requirement of the goal statement.

1.20—Ways and Means of Dealing with Specifics

1.21—Conventions

You will acquire knowledge of conventional outline form. Success will be determined by your ability to outline with 90% accuracy a list of 20 items with obvious degrees of subordination.

Critique:

I. Goal

A. Learner—You

B. Learning Task—

(1) Content—outline form

(2) Domain—Cognitive at 1.21 level (knowledge of conventional outline form)

(3) Future Time Orientation—will acquire

II. Behavioral Outcome (Evaluation)

Performance and criterion are congruent with the knowledge requirement of the goal statement.

1.22—Trends and Sequences

You will acquire a knowledge of the sequence of blood clotting, so that when given a list of the sequential steps of blood coagulation in mixed order, you will correctly number in writing and without error, each of the five steps in the order in which they actually occur in the clotting process.

Critique:

I. Goal

A. Learner—You

B. Learning Task—

(1) Content—blood clotting

(2) Domain—Cognitive at 1.22 level (knowledge of the sequence)

(3) Future Time Orientation—will acquire

II. Behavioral Outcome (Evaluation)

Performance and criterion are congruent with the knowledge requirement of the goal statement.

1.23—Classifications and Categories

Tenth grade chemistry students will acquire knowledge of the classifications of elements as evidenced by 90% of the students being able to orally distinguish between 35 given elements and correctly placing each element under its proper classification of gases or metals.

Critique:

I. Goal
  A. Learner Group—Tenth grade chemistry students
  B. Learning Task—
     (1) Content—classification of elements
     (2) Domain—Cognitive at the 1.23 level (knowledge of the classification)
     (3) Future Time Orientation—will acquire
II. Behavioral Outcome (Evaluation)
  Performance and criterion are congruent with the knowledge requirement of the goal statement.

1.24—Criteria

You must acquire a knowledge of the basic criteria used in judging the execution of the backhand spring. Success will be determined by your ability to identify in writing at least four of six criteria used in judgment of the stunt.

Critique:

I. Goal
  A. Learner—You
  B. Learning Task—
     (1) Content—execution of the backhand spring
     (2) Domain—Cognitive at 1.24 level (knowledge of the basic criteria used in judging)
     (3) Future Time Orientation—must acquire
II. Behavioral Outcome (Evaluation)
  Performance and criterion are congruent with the knowledge requirement of the goal statement.

1.25—Methodology

You will acquire knowledge of the different methods of passing a basketball. Success will be evidenced by your correctly matching with 100% accuracy, the names of nine methods of passing with their descriptions on a written test.

Critique:

I. Goal
  A. Learner—You
  B. Learning Task—
     (1) Content—passing a basketball
     (2) Domain—Cognitive at 1.25 level (knowledge of the different methods)
     (3) Future Time Orientation—will acquire
II. Behavioral Outcome (Evaluation)
  Performance and criterion are congruent with the knowledge requirement of the goal statement.

1.30—Universals and Abstractions in a Field

1.31—Principles and Generalizations

You should acquire an understanding at the knowledge level of the methods and basic principles of epidemiology, as they relate to community health nursing. Success in achieving this goal will be evidenced by your answering correctly at least 20 of 25 objective, short answer, and matching questions on a written examination developed by the instructor.
Critique:
  I. Goal
     A. Learner—You
     B. Learning Task—
        (1) Content—epidemiology
        (2) Domain—Cognitive at 1.31 level (understanding at the knowledge level of ... basic principles)
        (3) Future Time Orientation—should acquire
  II. Behavioral Outcome (Evaluation)
     Performance and criterion are congruent with the knowledge requirement of the goal statement.

1.32—Theories and Structures

You should become knowledgeable of the structure of a musical staff. Success will be determined by your ability to correctly draw and correctly number the lines and spaces on a staff without error.
Critique:
  I. Goal
     A. Learner—You
     B. Learning Task—
        (1) Content—musical staff
        (2) Domain—Cognitive at 1.32 level (become knowledgeable of the structure)
        (3) Future Time Orientation—should become
  II. Behavioral Outcome (Evaluation)
     Performance and criterion are congruent with the knowledge requirement of the goal statement.

In summing up the writing of behavioral objectives at the knowledge level, we find that the most important decision is to select an appropriate and meaningful goal and to state it in a manner that clearly indicates the classification level of the cognitive domain it represents. Once the understanding level is established, the teacher has no right to require any behavioral outcome or evaluation behavior from the student that is not congruent with the intent of the competency statement. Thus, all knowledge level objectives should be evaluated by behavioral outcomes which require only memory-recall type of information.

2.00—Comprehension

Objectives written at the comprehension level require that the learner give evidence to show that the message with which he/she is confronted is understood and that some use can be made of the ideas it contains. This is accomplished by the learner's ability to paraphrase, translate, interpret, or restate the ideas involved in the communication in some meaningful manner. The basic idea is to be able to discuss or communicate intelligently about something by responding to it in parallel form or by some simple extension of the ideas presented in the communication.

2.10—Translation

Translation enables the learner to make the transition of his/her understanding from the level of knowledge to the level of more complex behaviors. This involves a change from memory recall to the broader understanding of an entire concept. In translation, the learner can convert a communication from one language into another, replacing words by symbols, or any other conversions from one form of a message to an equivalent form.

Due to each person receiving a message within the framework of his/her own field of reference and within the context of a particular situation in which he/she is exposed to the message, translation becomes a semi-individualized type of response. Thus, each person will translate each communication based upon his/her own particular conception of what is a parallel or equivalent form.

Example Objective

Eleventh grade music history students will acquire comprehension of musical notation symbols, so that when given a list of 20 written definitions of symbols and 20 blank musical staves for notation, they will be able to translate the definitions into their symbolic notations with 80% accuracy on the written evaluation.

Critique:
I. Goal
  A. Learner Group—Eleventh grade music history students
  B. Learning Task—
    (1) Content—musical notation symbols
    (2) Domain—Cognitive at 2.10 level (comprehension indicates classification level two and is reinforced and placed into level 2.10 by the phrase "translate the definitions" in the evaluation component)
    (3) Future Time Orientation—will acquire
II. Behavioral Outcome (Evaluation)
  A. Performance—translating the definitions in writing
  B. Criterion Standard—80% accuracy
  C. Optional Statement—given a list of 20 written definitions of symbols and 20 blank musical staves for notation

The critique of this objective brings out the fact that the reader or user of an objective will see it as a whole, not as two component parts of a whole involving a competency or goal and a behavioral outcome. The most important characteristics of the objective are that the classification level be established, in so far as possible, in the goal and that the behavioral outcome be congruent with this requirement of the goal. It is relatively unimportant that the subcategory level be identified in each instance or whether it is identified as part of the goal component or by the behavioral outcome. The learner will simply view each objective as a whole with a purpose and method of showing success by evaluation.

This example objective requires not only memory or recall type of information, but, in addition, the learner must have the ability to convert definitions into parallel symbolic notation on a musical staff. There was no problem in placing it at the 2.10 classification level of the cognitive taxonomy.

2.20—Interpretation

Interpretation is similar to analysis in that the learner must not only be able to comprehend a communication through translation of its parts, but must understand the relationship of these parts and be able to tell the difference between the essential and non-essential portions of the communication. This involves the understanding of a message with reference to the arrangement of its parts and, if necessary, to be able to rearrange the component parts in his/her mind in order to make the meaning of the message more realistic. In some instances, interpretation will involve the interpretation of social data or the ability to make the proper qualifications when interpreting data.

Example Objective
Seventh grade industrial arts students will acquire comprehension of the basic safety rules for the home and the Industrial Arts Lab, so that when given ten practice situations related to the lab, the students will be able to correctly write out their interpretations of each situation as being safe or unsafe with at least 90% accuracy.
Critique:
    I. Goal
        A. Learner Group—Seventh grade industrial arts students
        B. Learning Task—
            (1) Content—basic safety rules for the home and the Industrial Arts Lab
            (2) Domain—Cognitive at 2.20 level (comprehension indicates classification level two and the sub-category is reinforced by the word "interpretations" in the evaluation component)
            (3) Future Time Orientation—will acquire
    II. Behavioral Outcome (Evaluation)
        A. Performance—writing out interpretations
        B. Criterion Standard—90% accuracy
        C. Optional Statement—given ten practice situations related to the lab

2.30—Extrapolation

Extrapolation, the third sub-category of comprehension, requires that the learner be able to make a type of inference by going from one proposition considered to be true to another whose truth is believed to follow that of the former. In other words, the learner must not only understand a message that is communicated to him/her, but should also be able to infer some logical consequences that might be expected to occur as a natural result of the truth of the first communication.

Extrapolation requires that the learner have knowledge of, be able to translate and interpret a communication, and, in addition, be able to extend the trends or tendencies beyond the given data by determining the implications and consequences. This means the learner will be able to make inferences, draw conclusions, predict trends, and make estimates and predictions.

Example Objective
You will acquire skill in determining the therapeutic measures needed to treat patients with fluid and electrolyte disturbances. Given the case history of a patient with both fluid and electrolyte disturbances, ten statements concerning potential treatments, and a three column answer sheet to indicate whether each statement is: (1) true, (2) insufficient data, or (3) false, you will correctly choose the right answer for at least eight of the ten statements.
Critique:
  I. Goal
    A. Learner—You (objective taken from a competency module identifying the student reader as the learner)
    B. Learning Task—
      (1) Content—therapeutic measures needed to treat patients with fluid and electrolyte disturbances
      (2) Domain—Cognitive at 2.30 level (the phrase "skill in determining" was used in lieu of the word comprehension in the objective as another way to indicate classification level. In this instance, the sub-category level was determined by interpreting the requirements of the total objective statement.)
      (3) Future Time Orientation—will acquire
  II. Behavioral Outcome (Evaluation)
    A. Performance—marking answers on a three column answer sheet
    B. Criterion Standard—correctly choosing eight out of ten statements
    C. Optional Statement—given the case history of a patient ..., ten statements ..., and a three column answer sheet

In this objective, we see for the first time the use of the word skill to indicate the cognitive classification level. Due to factors concerning the lack of knowledge of prior experiences of students which makes the classification of an objective as being a skill or an ability very difficult, skills and abilities are used synonymously in the taxonomy. However, it takes knowledge plus skills to equal abilities. For this reason, and for the purpose of simplifying the identification of the taxonomic levels, the author proposes to use the term skill to indicate comprehension, level two, or application, level three only. The distinction between these two levels when the term skill is used will be determined by the context in which this term is used and by analysis of the total understanding and behaviors required by the entire objective statement.

In summing up comprehension, we find that it involves the paraphrasing, translating, interpretation, inferring, or restating of ideas from one form of communication to another. Many additional terms, such as classifying, describing, illustrating, estimating, summarizing, explaining, transforming, reordering, predicting, and extending, can also be very helpful in not only more fully understanding this classification level, but also in writing the behavioral outcome statements used to evaluate competencies.

3.00–Application

The application category requires the learner to demonstrate the ability to make a transfer of his/her knowledge, comprehension, and experiences through comparison, implication, or numerical reference. It is closely related to comprehension, but goes one step further. In comprehension, a learner can solve a problem provided he/she is given a prescription for solving the problem and has been shown how to use the prescription. In application, the learner can solve the problem in an appropriate situation without having to be given the prescription for the problem solution.

For example, substitution of new numbers into a math formula or problem does not qualify as application because the problem is not a new one, but just different numbers. Application would require a student to study the problem and/or problem situation in order to determine what formula and prescription to use and then to correctly solve the problem.

Application requires the learner to use his/her knowledge and comprehension of an abstraction in practical situations which the learner did not encounter as part of his/her learning process. To do this, the learner may need to search a problem for familiar elements, to restructure the problem situation, and then, to transfer his/her previous training in a manner that best enables him/her to reach an acceptable problem solution or to use the appropriate variables in a correct manner.

In a classroom situation, such as accounting, geometry, music, art, research, etc., students may learn many definitions, principles, relationships, and other information on a day-by-day basis. Then, on a final examination, they may be given a practical problem that is new to the class. They will be expected to bring into focus the knowledge, comprehension, and other experiences they have obtained and to apply them in a manner that will achieve a correct problem solution.

The taxonomy specifies that there are at least two types of variations in application problems, those that require changes in behavior and those that require new situations. Behavioral application variations include the demonstration of the choice of correct principles, such as: (1) principles of psychology in identification of the features of a new social situation; (2) relating principles of democracy to current events; and (3) applying the principles or laws of trigonometry to every-day situations. New situations may include the use of simulated situations, the use of materials new to the learners, the application of new solutions to established situations, and/or the ability to apply scientific principles, theorems, or other abstractions to new situations.

Example Objective
Eleventh grade United States history students will develop the ability to apply the principles of the law of supply and demand to any market situation, so that when given a written test consisting of short descriptions of

25 economic situations, the students will correctly classify at least 20 as inflationary or deflationary.

Critique:

    I. Goal

        A. Learner Group—Eleventh grade United States history students

        B. Learning Task—

            (1) Content—principles of the law of supply and demand

            (2) Domain—Cognitive at 3.00 level (ability to apply to any market situation)

            (3) Future Time Orientation—will develop

    II. Behavioral Outcome (Evaluation)

        A. Performance—classifying on a written test

        B. Criterion Standard—correctly classify at least 20 out of 25

        C. Optional Statement—none

Example Objective

Home Economics I—Foods students will develop skill in applying the art of food preparation for best nutrient conservation. Given the principles for conservation for each food group, all students will prepare one food from each group completely without error, according to the following criteria:

Meat group—

    1. Cook at low temperature

    2. Cook only until done

    3. Follow directions for the particular type of meat used (poultry, fish, beef, etc.)

Fruits and Vegetables group—

    1. Do not allow the fruit to be exposed to the air excessively

    2. Cook in as large a size as possible

    3. Fruits and vegetables cooked in water are not drowned

    4. Cook in skins when possible

    5. Cook only until done and not beyond

Breads group—

    1. Use recipe given on biscuits

    2. Do not overmix or handle too much

    3. Cook only until done

Milk group—

    1. Use in a dessert such as puddings

    2. Cook at a low temperature and carefully

Critique:

    I. Goal

        A. Learner Group—Home Economics I—Foods students

        B. Learning Task—

            (1) Content—art of food preparation for best nutrient conservation

(2) Domain—Cognitive at 3.00 level (skill in applying)
(3) Future Time Orientation—will develop
II. Behavioral Outcome (Evaluation)
A. Performance—preparing one food from each of the four food groups
B. Criterion Standard—achieve each of the listed criteria for preparing the food without error
C. Optional Statement—given the principles for conservation for each food group

There are no sub-categories for application. These two example objectives illustrate the use of both the terms ability and skill as the method for identifying the classification level. As stated previously, we will use the word skill to identify the classification level of either comprehension or application. Application is the only level at which we will use either skill or ability. The reason is because this classification level is easier to identify due to the terms, such as apply, use, solve, predict, demonstrate, etc., that can be associated with the terms skill and ability, which make errors in classification less likely to occur.

At all of the higher classification levels, only the term ability or the term which identifies the classification level itself will be used. In each of the application level examples cited, the term skill or ability was followed by the term apply or applying, which served as a strong classification indicator. These two objectives also illustrate two widely different formats for stating the behavioral outcome component of the objective. The primary emphasis of application is for the learner to show that he/she can use what is learned. The important thing is for the learner to develop the ability to apply learning in new situations or to real-life situations.

4.00—Analysis

Analysis requires that the learner use conscious effort in demonstrating that he/she has the perception or insight to select the most important points in the material that have been presented. He/she should not only be able to identify the component parts of a whole, but also to understand the reasons for their relationships. As was true in the previous three classification levels, the use of classification level four also requires the utilization of levels one, two, and three.

Objectives in this classification are concerned with the meaning or intent of subject matter, such as is shown by a student's ability to: (1) distinguish relevant from non-essential material; (2) distinguish dominant from subordinate ideas; (3) distinguish the underlying purposes of a message; and (4) distinguish facts from assumptions or values. Analysis objectives contain many of the same ingredients as do comprehension and application objectives and are sometimes difficult to distinguish from objectives in levels two and three.

The key to analysis level objectives is that they can require more formal solutions and more conscious organization on the part of the learner in order to reach the solution to each problem. Analysis is essential to the performance of evaluation, but does not imply that a person can make evaluative judgments, as is the case with classification level six. There are three sub-categories in the Analysis classification, which involve the analysis of: (1) elements, 4.10; (2) relationships, 4.20; and (3) organization, 4.30.

4.10–Analysis of Elements

Analysis of elements requires the learner to distinguish between the important elements of any communication, whether they are implied, inferred, assumed, or explicitly stated. Elements may consist of facts, values, intents, assumptions, and conclusions which have been drawn. For example, the learner should be able to distinguish among (1) facts and values, (2) facts and intents, and (3) facts and assumptions.

Example Objective
You must develop the ability to make an analysis of the elements of a short story, so that when given an unfamiliar short story to read, you will be able to prepare, in a minimum of one paragraph each, a written analysis

in which you correctly identify the character, plot, setting, theme, and point of view of the author without error.

Critique:

I. Goal
   A. Learner—You
   B. Learning Task—
      (1) Content—elements of a short story
      (2) Domain—Cognitive at 4.10 level (identified by the phrase "ability to make an analysis of the elements")
      (3) Future Time Orientation—must develop

II. Behavioral Outcome (Evaluation)
   A. Performance—prepare a written analysis
   B. Criterion Standard—correctly identify without error
   C. Optional Statement—so that when given an unfamiliar short story to read

The term ability rather than the term skill will be used as an aid for indicating the classification level of all objectives in classification levels four, five, and six. This term along with sub-category indicators and indicators of behavioral outcomes to be performed in evaluation should suffice—along with the appropriateness and congruency found in each total objective statement—to classify all ability level objectives.

In the example objective stated, the learner was required to recognize the important elements of a short story. Elements such as the plot, theme, and point of view of the author may not be explicitly stated, which would require a carefully organized critical analysis of the book's content in order to meet the no error criterion established in the objectives evaluation component.

4.20—Analysis of Relationships

Once the learner has identified the different elements within a message, he/she may wish to determine some of the significant relationships between these elements. Any relationship which is important in context of the unit of instruction being investigated can qualify for this type of analysis. Some relationships will be quite simple, whereas, others may be much more difficult. An example might be the relationships found between elements which are essential to the communication and elements which are optional. In research, one may wish to analyze the relationships between the assumptions, hypotheses, and conclusions of a study.

Example Objective

You will develop the ability to analyze the relationships of compositional elements in the German lieder of Schubert and Brahms. Success will be determined by your ability to listen to a short work of one of these composers, and on a written essay test, correctly analyze the relationship of five out of seven of the following parameters:

(1) tonal consistency
(2) harmonic complexity
(3) melodic contour
(4) text painting
(5) accompaniment congruence with text
(6) rhythmic congruence with text
(7) romantic characteristics (literary) of text

Critique:

I. Goal
   A. Learner—You
   B. Learning Task—
      (1) Content—compositional elements in the German lieder of Schubert and Brahms
      (2) Domain—Cognitive at 4.20 level (identified by the phrase "ability to analyze the relationships of compositional elements")
      (3) Future Time Orientation—will develop
II. Behavioral Outcome (Evaluation)
   A. Performance—analyze on a written essay test
   B. Criterion Standard—correctly analyze five out of seven
   C. Optional Statement—probably none as stated, however, listening to a short work of one of these composers could be considered to be optional as a condition

4.30—Analysis of Organization

Objectives in this sub-category level can be difficult because the party producing a communication may not be consciously aware of the message's organizational principles himself/herself or they may be implied rather than explicitly stated. This sub-category involves objectives which may be concerned over the form, pattern, structure, or organization of the message being presented. The objectives may be concerned with the purposes, points of view, values, methods, etc., of an artist, a composer, or an author, as revealed in his/her creations. Concern can be given to how the elements of a creator's works are organized to produce the whole work. Art, music, and literature provide many opportunities for recognition of forms and patterns that are appropriate to this sub-category.

Example Objective

You will develop the ability to recognize the structural organization of a Shakespearean tragedy. Success will be determined by a written analysis of a tragedy you are assigned in which you can categorize the action of the tragedy into a given structure and, without error, determine the beginning and ending of each of the following: (1) exposition, (2) rising action, (3) falling action, (4) denouement, and (5) dramatic climax.
Critique:
  I. Goal
    A. Learner—You
    B. Learning Task—
      (1) Content—organization of a Shakespearean tragedy
      (2) Domain—Cognitive at 4.30 level (ability to recognize the structural organization)
      (3) Future Time Orientation—will develop
  II. Behavioral Outcome (Evaluation)
    A. Performance—written analysis of a tragedy
    B. Criterion Standard—achieve the five stated criteria without error
    C. Optional Statement—none

Example Objective

Eleventh grade music history students will develop the ability to recognize the structural organization of sonata-allegro form. Success will be determined by a written analysis of the first movement of a classical piano sonata in which they are to correctly outline the composer's framework (with key relationships and measure numbers) according to the sonata-allegro format: (1) Exposition; (2) Development, and (3) Recapitulation.
Critique:
  I. Goal
    A. Learner Group—Eleventh grade music history students
    B. Learning Task—
      (1) Content—structural organization of sonata-allegro form

> (2) Domain—Cognitive at 4.30 level (ability to recognize the structural organization)
> (3) Future Time Orientation—will develop

II. Behavioral Outcome (Evaluation)
   A. Performance—written analysis
   B. Criterion Standard—correctly outline according to the three criteria stated
   C. Optional Statement—none

In summing up the analysis classification level, 4.00, we find that students should be able to demonstrate that they have the insight or perception to pick out the significant elements or points in any material or communication with which they are presented. In addition, they should be able to detect relationships between the parts and also in relation to the whole message that is presented. Terms such as distinguish, contrast, derive, organize, discriminate, differentiate, discover, detect, deduce, categorize, and analyze are among the action words that can be helpful indicators for this classification level.

5.00—Synthesis

Synthesis means to combine diverse parts or elements so as to form a whole entity. This classification level requires learners to create a whole from component parts by being imaginative in producing a unique product. Sometimes synthesis is referred to as the level of understanding designed for creativity. This is because the learner is expected to develop something original. Originality in this instance does not mean something original that has never been accomplished before, but rather that the learner will create something that is new to himself/herself.

In order to fulfill the understanding requirements at this level, students must not be too structural in their thinking and must have the maximum opportunity to be individually independent. Since all learners can use their imaginations, synthesis objectives can be provided for students of all age groups. These types of objectives are designed to make students inquisitive and can become highly motivational.

Objectives at this level involve comprehension, application, and analysis, but, in addition, require originality. For this reason, some synthesis level objectives are more difficult to state with criteria, since too much emphasis upon some criteria can diminish the amount of creative thinking that a student may do. Thus, the learner must be given a great degree of freedom of response in accomplishing the goal of each objective.

5.10—*Production of a Unique Communication*

This sub-category attempts to communicate ideas, experiences, and feelings to other people in a manner that can be meaningful and appreciated by all parties. According to the taxonomy, the ability to write stories, essays, poems, etc., creatively; to make extemporaneous speeches; to tell of personal experiences; and to organize one's ideas into musical compositions and works of art are examples of objectives which may fit into this sub-category.

Example Objective

You will develop the ability to compose a sonnet. Success will be determined by your writing an original sonnet that correctly meets, according to teacher judgment, the following criteria:

  (1) contains 14 lines
  (2) written in iambic pentameter
  (3) contains three, four line quatrains
  (4) different aspect of theme must be developed in each quatrain
  (5) the final couplet must summarize the theme

Critique:
  I. Goal
    A. Learner—You
    B. Learning Task—
      (1) Content—an original sonnet
      (2) Domain—Cognitive at 5.10 level (the ability to compose a sonnet is one form of creating)
      (3) Future Time Orientation—will develop
  II. Behavioral Outcome (Evaluation)
    A. Performance—writing an original sonnet

B. Criterion Standard—correctly meets five stated criteria according
to teacher judgment
C. Optional Statement—none

5.20—Production of a Plan or Proposed Set of Operations

Objectives in this sub-category not only require that something
be produced that is original, but also specify that the entity created will be a plan or some other proposed set of operations that
will be carried out by someone. Thus, the creation that is produced should be something that will satisfy the requirements of
a specific task.

Synthesis objectives are, in a sense, the reverse of analysis objectives. In analysis we break a whole down into component parts,
whereas in synthesis we take parts and create a whole. It makes little difference as to whether the specifics of the assigned task are
furnished to the learner or if he/she develops them himself/herself.

Synthesis objectives in this sub-category will likely include:
(1) ways of testing hypotheses; (2) plans to solve a problem; (3) a
plan for teaching a particular unit of instruction; (4) miscellaneous
designs for hardware to perform specific functions; and (5) design-
ing buildings to given specifications.

Example Objective

You will develop the ability to design a plan of care for a patient with
fluid and electrolyte imbalances. Given a specific format for a nursery care
plan and a procedure for obtaining the patient's medical history, you will
create a written plan that correctly achieves each of the following criteria,
according to teacher judgment:

(1) adequacy of the data collecting process including a complete history of the patient's condition
(2) appropriateness of the problem list formulated from the patient's
history
(3) appropriateness of the nursing actions taken to solve the stated
problems
(4) documentation of actions with scientific principles obtained from
any source (books, articles, films) used

Critique:
- I. Goal
  - A. Learner—You
  - B. Learning Task—
    - (1) Content—plan for a patient with fluid and electrolyte imbalances
    - (2) Domain—Cognitive at 5.20 level (ability to design a plan of care requires creativity for a proposed set of operations to be carried out)
    - (3) Future Time Orientation—will develop
- II. Behavioral Outcome (Evaluation)
  - A. Performance—creating a written plan
  - B. Criterion Standard—correctly achieving each of four specified criteria according to teacher judgment
  - C. Optional Statement—given a specific format for a nursery care plan and a procedure for obtaining the patient's medical history

5.30—Derivation of a Set of Abstract Relations

This sub-category includes two different types of tasks. First, there are those in which the learner begins with concrete data which he/she must bring together to classify or explain. This can be purely explanatory or require something, such as the formulation of a hypothesis that will account for certain data that has been specified.

Second, the learner may begin with certain basic propositions or relations. This would require that the learner be somewhat restricted in his/her opportunities and that he/she operate from within some prescribed boundaries, such as the limits imposed by a particular theory. The originality and creativity is complete only as long as he/she does not go outside the prescribed boundaries.

According to the taxonomy, sub-category level 5.30 refers to the development of hypotheses, formulation of new theories, development of new conceptual structures, and the ability to make mathematic discoveries and generalizations. There are many problems that may be encountered in writing and using behavioral objectives at the synthesis level. These problems include: (1) providing conditions that permit freedom of expression; (2) providing time for creativity to develop and be recognized; (3) using subjective standards and teacher judgment in creative objectives where objective standards are neither available nor appropriate; (4) securing adequate sampling to insure that each product is truly indicative of the learner's ability; and (5) avoiding errors developing in the learner's understanding of the whole problem and its component parts.

Example Objective

Research I students should develop the ability to formulate hypotheses for use in experimental educational research. Given the statement of a specific problem, the problem rationale, a review of literature, and five general assumptions, students will be able to write out two testable hypotheses, one each under the hypothesis-prediction and the null hypothesis forms. Each hypothesis will meet all of the following criteria:

    (1) it is clearly worded in operational terms
    (2) it must be capable of being refuted
    (3) it is specific and testable
    (4) it is directly related to empirical phenomena
    (5) it is designed so that its test will provide an answer related to the original problem or purpose of the study
    (6) it should be related to available techniques of research design and statistical analysis

Critique:

  I. Goal

    A. Learner Group—Research I students

    B. Learning Task—

      (1) Content—hypotheses for use in experimental educational research

      (2) Domain—Cognitive at 5.30 level (ability to formulate hypotheses implies an abstract relationship)

      (3) Future Time Orientation—should develop

  II. Behavioral Outcome (Evaluation)

    A. Performance—writing out hypotheses

    B. Criterion Standard—achieving all of the six criteria stated according to the teacher's judgment

    C. Optional Statement—given the statement of a specific problem, the problem rationale, a review of literature, and five general assumptions

Analysis of the synthesis classification level has revealed that the learner must develop the ability to show that he/she can create new or original ideas from combinations of concepts. The ability to demonstrate originality in assembling separate elements into a whole entity is of paramount importance. This can be accomplished by objectives designed to give the learner the opportunity to: (1) be original; (2) develop abstract relationships such as hypotheses; (3) choose alternative courses of action in given situations; and (4) design experiments or other unique methods of expressing himself/herself as an individual. Action words, such as create, compose, organize, construct, design, plan, originate, predict, modify, produce, derive, synthesize, and formulate, can become useful indicators of objectives that are stated at the synthesis level.

6.00—Evaluation

Evaluation, the highest level of understanding presented in the taxonomy, requires the learner to make judgments and evaluate ideas, information, problem solutions, and procedures. In addition, he/she may render judgments concerning the value of various concepts relating to facts, opinions, and values. In order to perform at this level, the learner must have and be able to use knowledge, comprehension, application, analysis, and synthesis level understanding in forming the assessments he/she is required to make.

The judgments required in this sub-category may be either quantitative or qualitative or they may be objective or subjective. Since it is the thinking or understanding level that is of chief concern in evaluation level objectives, subjective judgment is perhaps preferable, since making judgments must always require some subjectivity.

Evaluation involves the use of some type of criteria in determining the worth of any given variable. Evaluation includes the use of values and the rendering of value judgments which relate the cognitive domain with the affective domain. Evaluation implies the determination of the quality or value of something; thus, appropriate criteria or values should be established that can be used to compare various facts, opinions, and other data in order to make judgments concerning them. In short, the primary concern of the evaluation classification level is to make judgments based upon either factual information or values. There are two sub-categories in the evaluation classification as follows:

6.10—Judgment in Terms of Internal Evidence

Evaluation in the first sub-category is concerned with internal criteria, such as evidence that will establish whether something is logically accurate or consistent with whatever it is supposed to represent. This can be interpreted to mean that an assessment is made to determine whether an object, creation, or thing has any flaws.

Evaluation at this level may be aided if one would ask himself/herself the following questions: (1) Is the work accurate?, (2) Has the creator been consistent in his/her use of terms?, (3) Are the ideas coherent?, and (4) Are the conclusions of the work logical based upon the material that was presented? In general, judgments in terms of internal evidence refer to: (1) the ability to discover logical inconsistencies on controversial issues; (2) the ability to assess something based upon the criteria set up for its existence; and (3) the ability to judge the accuracy of a message based upon whatever evidence is available at the time.

Example Objective

You should develop the ability to appraise the qualifications of two candidates seeking the same position, so that when given specific criteria for candidate selection, the necessary vitae, and enough time and money to further validate each candidate's credentials, you will be able to make a written recommendation that logically supports the candidate of your choice.

Critique:

    I. Goal

       A. Learner—You

    B. Learning Task—
      (1) Content—the qualifications of two candidates seeking the same position
      (2) Domain—Cognitive at 6.10 level (the ability to appraise—the sub-category is confirmed by the specific criteria given for candidate selection)
      (3) Future Time Orientation—should develop
  II. Behavioral Outcome (Evaluation)
    A. Performance—written recommendation
    B. Criterion Standard—logical support that is acceptable to the teacher
    C. Optional Statement—so that when given specific criteria for candidate selection, the necessary vitae, and enough time and money to further validate each candidate's credentials

6.20—Judgment in Terms of External Evidence

External evidence means that judgments are made based upon the ends to be served, standards which have been set, or by comparison of a work with other works in the field which are of the same classification. All works are assumed to be members of a class and, as such, must be judged by criteria appropriate for that class or by comparison with other works in the same classification.

Judgments in regard to ends to be achieved can be complex. An example might be judgments made on the basis of both effectiveness and efficiency. A particular work may be the most effective way to achieve a desired goal, but in so doing, it is so inefficient that the cost in time, material, and human resources virtually prohibits use of the work. In this instance, which end will take precedence over the other must be determined. In other words, is the end of effectiveness more important than the end of efficiency?

In some instances, this sub-category may require the learner to know a certain phenomenon well enough to organize his/her own criteria which will be appropriate for judging it. In general, students can make judgments by external criteria by: (1) using external standards; (2) weighing the pros and cons of alternative actions; and (3) the ability to use self-developed (aesthetic) standards in the choice of ordinary objects in his/her every-day environment.

Example Objective

Graduate students should develop the ability to evaluate the "goals approach" technique for writing behavioral objectives. Given an opportunity to research both the "goals approach" and the "outcomes approach" behavioral objective-writing techniques, students will be able to make a written comparison between the "goals approach" and the "outcomes approach," select their preference, and logically support their decision based upon their own conceptions of the ends which are best served by the methods they have chosen.

Critique:

I. Goal

   A. Learner Group—Graduate students

   B. Learning Task—

      (1) Content—the "goals approach" technique for writing behavioral objectives

      (2) Domain—Cognitive level 6.20 (the ability to evaluate, combined with confirmation of this level by the comparison of the two approaches based upon the ends to be served in the evaluation component)

      (3) Future Time Orientation—should develop

II. Behavioral Outcome (Evaluation)

   A. Performance—to make a written comparison

   B. Criterion Standard—logically supporting their preference which is established by teacher approval of both their choice and their logic

   C. Optional Statement—given an opportunity to research both the "goals approach" and the "outcomes approach" behavioral objective-writing techniques

In this objective, the students would be required to analyze both objective-writing approaches and form conclusions concerning which of the two would best meet the ends to be served. This would need to be conveyed to the teacher in a logical written presentation.

Example Objective

You will develop the ability to make an evaluation of one movement of a Romantic symphony based on widely accepted aesthetic standards. Success will be determined by your ability, according to teacher judgment, to incorporate aesthetic standards into a five-page paper evaluating one movement of a symphony without quotation or paraphrase of published critiques. One of the following works may be selected:

Brahms: Symphony No. 4, op. 98, first movement
Tchaikovsky: Symphony No. 6, op. 74, first movement
Berlioz: Symphonie Fantastique
Strauss: Till Eulenspiegel's Merry Pranks
Critique:
I. Goal
  A. Learner—You
  B. Learning Task—
    (1) Content—one movement of a Romantic symphony
    (2) Domain—Cognitive at 6.20 level (the ability to make an evaluation on widely accepted aesthetic standards)
    (3) Future Time Orientation—will develop
II. Behavioral Outcome (Evaluation)
  A. Performance—writing a five-page paper
  B. Criterion Standard—achieving the content criteria of the five-page paper according to teacher judgment
  C. Optional Statement—none

This objective needed no assistance from its behavioral outcome in clearly indicating the sub-category classification level in the competency statement or goal component of the objective. There are many terms, such as argue, prove, assess, judge, select, evaluate, weigh values, appraise, compare, contrast, and validate, which can become good indicator words for use in the evaluation level classification.

Summary

This chapter has illustrated the value of critiquing objectives as they are being written to determine if they are appropriate for the use that is to be made of them. The reader should keep in mind that such critiques are intended to be mental activities only and will never occur in written form except as a training exercise used when students are first learning to write behavioral objectives.

One must also keep in mind that the primary target to whom the teacher needs to communicate is himself/herself. True, the learner will eventually need to understand and benefit from use of the objectives. The teachers, however, must first clearly understand the target or competencies upon which they should focus. It is the teachers who will prepare the enabling strategies and decide how evaluation to determine success in competency attainment will be measured. This can best be accomplished by teachers writing and critiquing each objective they intend to use in order to bring the most relevant experiences into the classroom situation.

The chapter further developed the technique for writing competency statements by use of the cognitive taxonomy. This was accomplished by first establishing the cognitive domain as containing six classification levels of understanding and then using specific indicator words and phrases to identify the classification level of behavior for which each competency is designed. The term knowledge was chosen as the proper indicator for level one. The terms comprehension and skill are used to identify level two, whereas, either the term skill or ability was designated for use at level three, application. The three highest level classifications, analysis, synthesis, and evaluation, were all limited to use of the term ability as the primary indicator expression.

The rationale for the selection of these terms is quite simple. First, there is only one knowledge level classification and the word knowledge is the most specific manner in which that classification level can be identified. The term acquire was used as the indicator for future time orientation at classification level one. This is because a person is not born with knowledge. Therefore, information at this level must be acquired.

The terms comprehension and skill were used at level two due to comprehension being the name of the classification level and since skill is a less complex behavior than ability; thus, this term is used at level two, which is the lowest complex behavior level. Again, the term acquire was used to identify future time orientation with the term comprehension. However, future time orientation is identified by the term develop whenever the terms skill or ability are used. The reason for this change in wording is that the acquisition of skills and abilities requires experiences in addi-

Figure 8.2. Format for writing competency statements according to classification levels of the cognitive taxonomy.

UNDERSTANDING

| 1.00 | KNOWLEDGE | — The learner will acquire knowledge |

2.00 COMPREHENSION
- The learner will acquire comprehension
- The learner will develop skill

3.00 APPLICATION
- The learner will develop skill
- The learner will develop ability
- The learner will develop an understanding at the Application level

4.00 ANALYSIS
- The learner will develop the ability
- The learner will develop an understanding at the Analysis level

5.00 SYNTHESIS
- The learner will develop the ability
- The learner will develop an understanding at the Synthesis level

6.00 EVALUATION
- The learner will develop the ability
- The learner will develop an understanding at the Evaluation level

tion to knowledge and experiences or combinations of knowledge and skill.

Graphically speaking, the format recommended for writing competency statements according to the classification levels of the cognitive taxonomy is as depicted in Figure 8.2.

Finally, the reader should recognize that only a cursory coverage of the content of the cognitive taxonomy can be outlined in one chapter of this text. There are many valuable aids to be found in the taxonomy other than just the outline of the classification levels. One example is the sample test items that are provided as representative of questions that can be asked which include all classification and sub-category levels of the taxonomy. *It is recommended that teachers who intend to involve themselves in depth in working at various levels of the cognitive domain should own and use a copy of the taxonomy itself as a means of furthering their expertise in this area.*

Note

1. Benjamin S. Bloom *et al. Taxonomy of Educational Objectives: The Classification of Educational Goals: Handbook I: Cognitive Domain* (New York: Longman, Inc., 1956).

IX.

Writing Behavioral Objectives for Different Classification Levels of the Psychomotor Taxonomy

"One must always keep in mind that behavior may be conceptualized as falling into one of three learning domains, but in reality when observing a child's behavior it is usually a combination of all three."

—Harrow[1]

CHAPTER GOALS

The reader should:

1. acquire comprehension of Harrow's[2] *Taxonomy of the Psychomotor Domain**;
2. develop skill in writing behavioral objectives at various classification levels of the psychomotor taxonomy.

The taxonomy of the psychomotor domain is perhaps the most functional and the easiest of the three behavioral taxonomies to

*Adapted from *A TAXONOMY OF THE PSYCHOMOTOR DOMAIN: A GUIDE FOR DEVELOPING BEHAVIORAL OBJECTIVES*, by Anita J. Harrow. Copyright © 1972 by Longman, Inc. Permission granted by Longman.

use as a guideline for developing behavioral objectives. First, it was conceptualized from the beginning as a tool to be used in goal setting to determine appropriate competencies. Second, all examples of objectives written in the taxonomy are stated according to the "goals approach" objective-writing technique. This better insures that any enabling strategies designed to achieve the objectives will focus upon the competency to be achieved, not upon the behavioral outcome or the evaluation performance. Third, the primary emphasis upon goal (competency) development and the ease in which many psychomotor behavioral outcomes can be overtly observed insure that each competency will be relatively specific and more likely to be evaluated correctly with specifically observable behavioral outcomes.

Eiss and Harbeck[3] supported this third point when they wrote, "It is only in the psychomotor that the credibility gap is fairly close between behavior and objective." They referred to this credibility gap as being the lack of certainty that overt measurable learner behaviors, often identified as sample evaluation indicators, should be accepted as evidence that the goal of an objective has been achieved.

The term psychomotor means mind-movement. Harrow[4] has operationally defined the term psychomotor to mean "observable, voluntary, human motion." This definition distinguishes between the two major categories of movement, involuntary movements and voluntary movements. Thus, the taxonomy is not primarily concerned with involuntary movements and recognizes them only in the sense that they are essential to life and form a prerequisite foundation upon which voluntary movements can be developed. Figure 9.1 illustrates these two major categories of movement.

In this illustration, classification level 1.00, involuntary reflex movement, is shown to contain two major divisions: spinal reflexes and suprasegmental reflexes. These movements occur automatically according to stimulation and without learning. These movement responses can be considered to be innate abilities that,

Figure 9.1. Two major categories of movement.

Voluntary Purposeful Observable Human Movement		2.0—Basic Fundamental Movement A. Locomotor B. Non-Locomotor C. Manipulative

Involuntary Movement	1.00—Reflex Movement
	A. Spinal Reflexes
	  1. Segmented
	  2. Intersegmented
	
	B. Suprasegmental Reflexes	

in normal children are functional at birth, develop through maturation, and occur involuntarily as far as mind control is concerned. Obviously, this type of movement cannot be learned and cannot be considered as a level at which competencies or objectives should be stated. The second classification level, 2.00, basic fundamental movement, includes locomotor, non-locomotor, and manipulative types of movement. Adaptations and variations of the basic fundamental movements are necessary in the development of movement activities at the higher classification levels.

Figure 9.2 illustrates the six levels of the taxonomy and the principal types of response or responses that are of primary concern in each level.

Writing Objectives According to the Psychomotor Taxonomy Classification Levels

Writing objectives for the voluntary movement classification levels of the taxonomy can begin with level 2.00, basic fundamental movement, and includes all of the hierarchically arranged levels through level 6.00, non-discursive communication. It is not anticipated that many objectives will be written at either level 2.00 or level 6.00. In normal children, basic fundamental movement behaviors will occur naturally, beginning at birth. Level 6.00 behaviors are so complex and advanced that very few teachers will have students ready for this level of sophistication, which requires skilled movement as a prerequisite.

Learning to write psychomotor objectives by the "goals approach" technique is not difficult once the learner has used this approach to write objectives utilizing the cognitive taxonomy. The primary requirements are to first determine the learner's movement needs, relate these needs to the classification levels of the taxonomy, and then state the specific competencies to be obtained as goal statements. The taxonomy, itself, can serve as a guideline for conducting a needs assessment, if such an activity is necessary. Once a specific competency (goal) is stated, the final

Figure 9.2.   Taxonomy classification levels and the interplay of movement
              responses.

INVOLUNTARY MOVEMENT	VOLUNTARY PURPOSEFUL OBSERVABLE HUMAN MOVEMENT
1.00 — Reflex Movement — Innate abilities — Reflex Response (R)	
REFLEX MOVEMENT REPRESENTING THE PREREQUISITE FOUNDATION UPON WHICH VOLUNTARY MOVEMENT RESPONSE IS BASED	2.00 — Basic Fundamental Movement — Inherent movement patterns — Maturational Response (M)
	3.00 — Perceptual Abilities — Necessary for learning at the higher levels in all three domains — Maturation and Acquired Response (MA)
	4.00 — Physical Abilities — Necessary for efficiently functioning body — Maturation and Acquired Response (MA)
	5.00 — Skilled Movement — Complex Movement — Acquired Response (A)
	6.00 — Non-Discursive Communication — Creative or Interpretive Movement — Acquired Response (A)

step in writing each objective is to attach a behavioral outcome that can be used to indicate when success in competency achievement has been reached.

2.00—Basic Fundamental Movement

Objectives in this classification level are categorized under three major and two minor sub-categories, as shown in Figure 9.3.

Movement activities at this classification level begin at birth and are, primarily, developed by the learner on his/her own. It is these basic movement patterns that will later become the base for the development of the skilled movements referred to in classification level 5.00. Since maturation rather than acquired response is the primary prerequisite for the development of movement at this level, no example objectives will be given in this text. Students desiring to write objectives at this level are encouraged to secure a copy of the psychomotor taxonomy for their own personal use.

3.00—Perceptual Abilities

Harrow[5] stated that perception is the process of becoming aware, attending to, or interpreting stimuli. She further indicated that *perceptual abilities* include all of a learner's perceptual modalities where stimuli are received and carried to the higher brain centers for interpretation. According to the taxonomy, perceptual modalities include the following components: (1) kinesthetic, the feeling with reference to muscle sense; (2) visual, the seeing; (3) auditory, the hearing; (4) tactile, the differentiation by touching; and (5) the coordinated abilities, discernment by two or more of the perceptual modalities. The visual, auditory, and kinesthetic components can be considered to be the primary perceptual modalities.

Most behavioral objectives to be written under the classification of perceptual abilities will be stated under the sub-category heading of one of the three primary perceptual modalities or a com-

Figure 9.3. Sub-categories of basic fundamental movement, 2.00.

SUB-CATEGORY CLASSIFICATIONS	GENERAL DEFINITION	EXAMPLE MOVEMENT ACTIVITIES
2.10– Locomotor Movement	Changes the learner from a stationary to an ambulatory being	Walking, running, crawling, sliding, hopping, climbing, jumping, rolling, etc.
2.20– Non-Locomotor Movement	Creates movement patterns in space	Pushing, pulling, stretching, bending, twisting, stooping, free throw shooting, rope turning, etc.
2.30– Manipulative Movement	Coordinated movements of extremities	
2.31– Prehension	Combining of several reflexes and the coordination of the visual perceptual abilities with prehensive activity	Handling blocks, cups, balls, and using drawing implements, etc.
2.32– Dexterity	Quick, precise movements pertaining to hands and fingers	Tying shoes, buttoning buttons, etc.

bination of two or more of them. The sub-categories for each of the five modalities are identified in Figure 9.4.

Example Objective for Kinesthetic Discrimination (3.114)

Sixth grade children will improve their body balance in various positions, so that when given pre- and post-tests consisting of the opportunity to perform on the balance beam, they will be able to increase by at least one count, three of the following balances without any outside assistance: (1) v-seat; (2) knee scale; (3) ballet point; (4) lunge; and (5) one-leg squat.

Critique:

I. Goal
   A. Learner Group—Sixth grade children
   B. Learning Task—
      (1) Content—body balance in various positions
      (2) Domain—Psychomotor at 3.114 level (the word balance identifies the domain sub-category)
      (3) Future Time Orientation—will improve

II. Behavioral Outcome (Evaluation)
   A. Performance—performing balances on the balance beam
   B. Criterion Standard—increasing by at least one count at least three balances
   C. Optional Statement—none as stated to show improvement

Example Objective for Auditory Memory (3.33)

You will develop auditory memory in relation to piano concerti themes of Tchaikovsky and Grieg, and the violin concerti themes of Mendelssohn and Tchaikovsky. Success will be determined by your ability to correctly orally identify six out of eight themes from the following concerti:

Tchaikovsky: Violin Concerto in D Major, op. 35, first movement
Mendelssohn: Violin Concerto in e minor, op. 64, first movement
Tchaikovsky: Piano Concerto in Bb Major, op. 23, first movement
Grieg: Piano Concerto in a minor, op. 16, first movement

Critique:

I. Goal
   A. Learner—You
   B. Learning Task—
      (1) Content—auditory memory of piano and violin concerti themes
      (2) Domain—Psychomotor at 3.33 level (auditory memory)
      (3) Future Time Orientation—will develop

II. Behavioral Outcome (Evaluation)
   A. Performance—orally identify
   B. Criterion Standard—correctly identifying six out of eight themes
   C. Optional Statement—none

Figure 9.4. Sub-category designations for perceptual abilities, 3.00.

SUB-CATEGORY CLASSIFICATIONS	GENERAL DEFINITIONS

3.10— Kinesthetic Discrimination
  3.11— Body Awareness
    3.111— Bilaterality
    3.112— Laterality
    3.113— Sidedness
    3.114— Balance
 	
  3.12— Body Image
 	
  3.13 - Body Relationship to
    Surrounding Space
	Body sense which includes body awareness and the ability to recognize and control body appendages.

3.20— Visual Discrimination
  3.21— Acuity
  3.22— Tracking
  3.23— Memory
  3.24— Figure Ground Differentiation
  3.25— Perceptual Consistency
	The interpretation of stimulation entering the organism by way of the receptor cells of the eye and carried over the afferent pathways to the brain.

3.30— Auditory Discrimination
  3.31— Acuity
  3.32— Tracking
  3.33— Memory
	The interpretation of stimulation entering the organism by way of the receptor cells of the ear and carried over afferent pathways to the brain.

3.40— Tactile Discrimination	The ability to differentiate between textures by touching.

3.50— Coordinated Abilities
  3.51— Eye-hand coordination
  3.52— Eye-foot coordination
	Activities involving two or more of the perceptual abilities and movement patterns.

Additional Objectives Without Critique

1. Home economics students must develop the ability to distinguish between a nap fabric and a fabric without a nap so that when given ten fabric swatches to be identified through tactile discrimination, the students will orally identify at least nine correctly. (3.40)

2. You should develop the ability to distinguish rhyming sounds in words. Success in achieving this goal will be determined by your ability to raise your hand when you hear two rhyming words out of four as they are called orally by the teacher. This must be done successfully ten out of 20 times. (3.31)

3. Kindergarten children will develop eye-hand and eye-foot coordination. Success will be determined by each child's ability to achieve each of the following tasks:

(1) throw a ball into a hoop positioned ten feet from him/her in six out of ten attempts,

(2) bounce and catch a ball on the first bounce in seven out of ten times,

(3) dribble a ball with both hands without losing control of the ball for a distance of 15 feet,

(4) throw a ball more than five feet into the air and catch it in six out of ten times,

(5) straddle run a rope three times, arranged in three different zig-zag patterns, without touching the rope, and

(6) perform the paperwalk task for a distance of 30 feet in 60 seconds. (3.50)

4. You will be required to develop the eye-hand coordination necessary to form vertical, horizontal, and diagonal strokes and to form humps and inverted humps on strokes. Success will be evidenced by your ability to correctly perform each of the following:

(1) to copy in distinguishable form, and within primary lined paper, 80% of the letters that are composed of vertical and horizontal strokes such as L, l, I, E, F, T, t, and H;

(2) to copy in distinguishable form, in full height or half height on primary lined paper, at least 80% of the letters that are composed of diagonal strokes and/or in combination with straight lines such as K, k, Y, y, X, x, V, v, W, w, Z, z; and

(3) to print letters, either whole or half line size, that represent 80% of the letters composed of full and half line size humps such as: n, m, h, r, U, and u. (3.51)

One final note on perceptual abilities is that this classification level does not consist of purely voluntary movement activities. Some objectives, such as the example for auditory memory (3.33), also involve cognitive development as an additional consideration. It is a necessary classification, however, in order to aid in the transition of pure movement responses into perceptual motor activities which involve both the interpretation and motor response an individual makes to a stimulus.

Flinchum[6] described level 3.00, perceptual abilities, as building on to the previous stages of the taxonomy and said that it "adds another dimension, perception, prior to motor response. In this motor area, the child obtains sensory input, and interprets it before responding with a movement. It seems reasonable to assume that this is a very important area to develop."

4.00—Physical Abilities

Physical abilities are described in the taxonomy as being essential to the efficient functioning of a learner in the psychomotor domain and as a foundation upon which to develop skilled movements. Objectives written for this classification level can be categorized under four major and six minor sub-categories as shown in Figure 9.5.

Example Objective for Cardiovascular Endurance (4.12)
You will improve your cardiovascular endurance, so that when given the opportunity to take the one-minute cardiovascular endurance test on a pre- and post-test basis, you will increase the number of steps you can take by at least 20.
Critique:
   I. Goal
      A. Learner—You
      B. Learning Task—
         (1) Content—cardiovascular endurance
         (2) Domain—Psychomotor at 4.12 level
         (3) Future Time Orientation—will improve
  II. Behavioral Outcome (Evaluation)
      A. Performance—taking a pre- and post- one-minute cardiovascular endurance test
      B. Criterion Standard—increasing the number of steps on the post-test by at least 20
      C. Optional Statement—none

Figure 9.5. Sub-categories for physical abilities, 4.00.

SUB-CATEGORY CLASSIFICATIONS	GENERAL DEFINITIONS
4.10— Endurance 4.11— Muscular Endurance 4.12— Cardiovascular Endurance	The ability of the body to supply and utilize oxygen improving a learner's capacity to endure strenuous activity for longer periods of time while retaining efficiency in one's movement patterns.
4.20— Strength	The learner's ability to "exert tension against resistance."
4.30— Flexibility	The range of motion in one's joints a learner is able to achieve.
4.40— Agility 4.41— Change Direction 4.42— Stop and Start 4.43— Reaction-Response 4.44— Dexterity	The ability of a learner to move quickly in changing direction, starting, stopping, reaction time, and deftness in manipulative activities.

Additional Objectives Without Critique

1. You will improve your agility. Success will be determined by a pre- and post-test on the ability test explained in Section III of your handbook on which you should increase your score by at least 12 steps. (4.40)

2. You will improve your body suppleness and flexibility in the area of the lower back and leg as evidenced by your showing an increase of at least two inches on the box flexibility test given on a pre- and post-test basis. (4.30)

3. You will improve your abdominal strength as evidenced by your increasing by at least ten the number of sit-ups you can perform in a ten-minute period when evaluated on a pre- and post-test. (4.20)

4. You will improve your agility so that when administered a pre- and post-test of the A.A.H.P.E.R. shuttle run test, you will improve your score by at least 20%. (4.40)

5. You will improve your flexibility, so that when sitting, legs apart, you will be able to touch the floor with your head by bending forward. (4.30)

The reader will note that objectives one and four, as well as objectives two and five, represent the same sub-category classification levels respectively, agility and flexibility. This emphasizes that different teachers may not state objectives in the same area in the same manner and that any measure used for the statement of a behavioral outcome is just a sample of the many behavioral outcomes that are possible. Thus, the evaluation components for two common objectives can be somewhat different, and each one could be correct or adequate in the context of the situation in which it is used.

5.00—Skilled Movement

Skilled movements are made possible by the adaptation of the learner's inherent basic fundamental movement patterns in a manner that will result in the acquisition of a degree of efficiency when performing a complex movement task. These types of movements require learning, utilizing the learners' perceptual and physical abilities, and are, generally, considered to be reasonably complex.

The taxonomy uses two continuums, a vertical and a horizontal, to explain movement activities in this classification. The vertical continuum is used as the basis for assigning the hierarchical sub-categories. This continuum refers to the degree of difficulty of various movement skills or the levels of complexity of the movement behaviors. The horizontal continuum refers to the proficiency or levels of skill mastery achieved within each level of complexity. This classification level can be seen graphically in Figure 9.6.

The first requirement of writing objectives in this classification level is to determine whether the competency should be stated as a simple, compound, or complex adaptive skill. Then decide whether it involves a beginner, intermediate, advanced, or highly skilled learner group and write the competency and behavioral outcome accordingly.

Example Objective for Advanced Compound Adaptive Skill (5.23)
You will develop the ability to execute a chip shot with a pitching wedge as demonstrated by your ability to hit five of ten balls to a simulated green from 30 yards away within a 30-foot radius of the flag.
Critique:
  I. Goal
    A. Learner—You
    B. Learning Task—
      (1) Content—execute chip shot with pitching wedge
      (2) Domain—Psychomotor at 5.23 level (using a golf club indicates the use of a tool or implement)
      (3) Future Time Orientation—will develop
  II. Behavioral Outcome (Evaluation)
    A. Performance—hitting golf ball
    B. Criterion Standard—five of ten golf balls land and stay within a 30-foot radius of the flag
    C. Optional Statement—none
Additional Objectives Without Critique
1. You will develop skill in hitting the golf ball out of a sand trap as demonstrated by your ability to hit five of ten balls from a simulated sand trap ten yards from a simulated green into a 30-foot radius around the flag. (5.23)
2. You will develop skill in hitting power serves in tennis. Success will be determined by your ability to hit your first service at full speed so that it goes

Figure 9.6. The sub-categories of skilled movements, 5.00.

SUB-CATEGORY CLASSIFICATIONS	GENERAL DEFINITIONS	EXAMPLE ACTIVITIES
5.10— Simple Adaptive Skill 5.11— Beginner 5.12— Intermediate 5.13— Advanced 5.14— Highly Skilled	Involves the simple adaptation of inherent basic fundamental movement patterns into an acquired skills activity.	Dancing or waltzing, typing, piano playing, archery, etc.
5.20— Compound Adaptive Skill 5.21— Beginner 5.22— Intermediate 5.23— Advanced 5.24— Highly Skilled	Involves simple adaptation of inherent movement patterns and in addition requires the incorporation or management of some tool or implement.	Tennis, Golf, Fencing
5.30— Complex Adaptive Skill 5.31— Beginner 5.32— Intermediate 5.33— Advanced 5.34— Highly Skilled	Involves intricate manipulation of the body characterized by the body changing its base of support.	Gymnastics, aerial somersaults, diving

over the net and into the proper service court in seven of ten service attempts.
(5.24)

Example Objective for Advanced Complex Adaptive Skill (5.33)

You will be expected to develop skill in selected gymnastic events. Success
will be evidenced by your ability to perform a series of one front walkover,
one front cartwheel, two backward rolls, and one back handspring, and to receive from a panel of judges, a mark no lower than six on an eight point scale
for your performance on the exercise.

Critique:

I. Goal
   A. Learner—You
   B. Learning Task—
      (1) Content—selected gymnastic events
      (2) Domain—Psychomotor at 5.33 level (some of the activities re-
          quire a change in the performer's base of support)
      (3) Future Time Orientation—will be expected to develop

II. Behavioral Outcome (Evaluation)
   A. Performance—performance of a series of gymnastic movement skill
      activities
   B. Criterion Standard—judges rating of no lower than six on an eight
      point scale
   C. Optional Statement—none

Additional Objectives Without Critique

1. You will develop your ability to set the volleyball. Success will be determined by legally setting seven out of ten consecutive sets on the wall as determined by the subjective judgment of the instructor. (5.13)

2. You will develop your ability to serve the volleyball. Success will be
determined by scoring 35 out of 50 points on a serving test. (5.12)

3. You will develop dribbling skill with your dominant hand, so that when
five chairs are set up, six feet apart, you will be able to dribble the ball 30
feet, weaving in and out of the line of chairs and return in the same manner
within 25 seconds. (5.13)

4. You will develop skill in performing dismounts from the balance beam.
Success will be determined by your performing three of the following dismounts without falling: side seat, front vault, straddle jump, pike jump, and
jump 1/2 turn. (5.32)

5. You will develop skill in driving a golf ball from a tee using the number
one wood. Given an opportunity to drive ten balls with the number one
wood, you will hit at least five of them more than 150 yards and within a
boundary of 50 yards wide. (5.22)

The reader should note that for most practical purposes, it
should not be necessary to classify objectives for skilled movement

Figure 9.7. The sub-categories of non-discursive communication, 6.00.

SUB-CATEGORY CLASSIFICATIONS	GENERAL DEFINITIONS
6.10– Expressive Movement 6.11– Posture and Carriage 6.12– Gestures 6.13– Facial Expression 6.20– Interpretive Movement 6.21– Aesthetic Movement 6.22– Creative Movement	Movement expressions which are part of every person's movement repertoire, and movement interpolations which include any efficiently performed skilled movements and movement patterns designed to communicate a message to a viewer.

activities by the horizontal continuum designations as is shown in the sample objectives. The use of the 5.10, 5.20, and 5.30 sub-category classification designations should generally be sufficient.

6.00—Non-Discursive Communication

Non-discursive communication is composed of movement behaviors involving creativity, expression, and interpretation. Figure 9.7 illustrates this classification level.

Due to the many restrictions on the writing of behavioral objectives at this classification level, the author does not recommend it for use by educators except in rare instances, such as in the case of ballet and other very advanced dramatic presentations. For this reason, no example objectives will be stated for non-discursive communication. It is highly recommended that persons desiring to write objectives at level 6.00 secure their own copy of the psycho-motor taxonomy and study this classification level in depth.

Notes

1. Anita J. Harrow. *A Taxonomy of the Psychomotor Domain: A Guide for Developing Behavioral Objectives* (New York: Longman, Inc., 1972), p. 30.
2. *Ibid.*, pp. 1-185.
3. Albert F. Eiss and Mary Blatt Harbeck. *Behavioral Objectives in the Affective Domain* (Washington, D.C.: National Science Teachers Association, 1969), p. 4.
4. Anita J. Harrow. *A Taxonomy of the Psychomotor Domain: A Guide for Developing Behavioral Objectives* (New York: Longman, Inc., 1972), pp. 31, 45, 46, 152.
5. *Ibid.*, pp. 57, 163.
6. Betty M. Flinchum. *Motor Development in Early Childhood* (St. Louis: C. V. Mosby Company, 1975) p. 49.

X.

Writing Behavioral Objectives
in the Affective Domain

"At all levels of the affective domain, affective objectives have a cognitive component."

—Krathwohl[1]

"Next to excellence is the appreciation of it."

—Thackeray

"Our feelings were given us to excite to action, and when they end in themselves, they are cherished to no good purpose."

—Landford

CHAPTER GOALS
The reader should:
1. develop comprehension of Krathwohl's *Taxonomy of Educational Objectives: Affective Domain*;[2]
2. develop the ability to write behavioral objectives at selected classification levels of the affective taxonomy.*

---

*Adapted from *TAXONOMY OF EDUCATIONAL OBJECTIVES: THE CLASSIFICATION OF EDUCATIONAL GOALS: HANDBOOK 2: AFFECTIVE DOMAIN*, by David R. Krathwohl *et al.* Copyright © 1964 by Longman, Inc. Permission granted by Longman.

197

During the course of the behavioral objective movement, the need to write objectives in the affective domain has greatly exceeded the "know how" of most educators to formulate them. Mager's[3] outcomes objective-writing approach has not been very useful in stating affective objectives due to: (1) the inability of objectives stated in this manner to be able to stand on their own when isolated from the goal or purpose which they represent; (2) the apparent triviality that results from the statement of specific behaviors in isolation; and (3) the difficulty in identifying and stating overtly observable behaviors that can conclusively be said to be truly representative of the behaviors a person can be expected to exhibit as proof he/she has achieved a given affective competency.

Problems one and two, identified in the above paragraph, have been eliminated or greatly reduced by users of the goals objective-writing approach, but problems of affective objective evaluation still remain a primary concern of all persons developing behavioral objectives in the affective domain. Among the continuing problems of evaluation in this area are the following:

(1) identification of clear and specifically defined goals;
(2) inability to evaluate affective change at the higher levels immediately;
(3) the specification of evaluation indicators which are either too general (meaningless) or too specific delimiting the number of alternative behaviors that may be used;
(4) valid overtly observable and measurable behaviors are both hard to define and to observe;
(5) criterion standards may not always be available or appropriate for some behavioral outcomes used for evaluation purposes;
(6) the difficulty in observing student behaviors without the students being aware of the behavior desired by the evaluator; and

(7) the validity and reliability of many affective rating instruments are difficult to establish.

The Affective Taxonomy

The affective domain represents *the sphere* of influence that involves behaviors caused by feelings or emotions. It is only after full recognition of the many problems of affective evaluation and of the nebulous nature of the domain itself, that an objective writer can with much trepidation begin to write meaningful objectives in this area.

The affective taxonomy represents five hierarchical classification levels defined as follows:

1.00 — Receiving	— the level at which the learner develops an awareness of stimuli.
2.00 — Responding	— the level at which the learner can be expected to give his/her first positive reactions to stimuli.
3.00 — Valuing	— the level at which the learner may display behaviors that are consistent with a high degree of internalization and commitment.
4.00 — Organization	— the level at which the learner may be expected to organize his/her highly developed and frequently encountered feelings into a system of values.
5.00 — Characterization by a Value Complex	— the level at which the learner can be expected to display a high level of adjustment by re-

sponding in a similar fashion to value laden situations.

In addition to and closely associated with these classification levels and their corresponding sub-categories, the taxonomy portrays the following terms and the range of their meaning in relationship to the hierarchically stated classification levels:

1. Interest   — a perceptual condition combining both cognitive and affective consciousness into a type of feeling.

2. Appreciation — emotional awareness of the significance of something.

3. Attitudes   — emotionalized dispositions utilized in the information processing aspects of behavior which will cause a person to think or behave either positively or negatively toward a particular variable.

4. Values   — any quality or trait deemed worthy enough to be socially, morally, or psychologically desirable.

5. Adjustment   — the adaptation of a person which will enable him/her to deal more effectively with his/her environment.

The structure of the affective taxonomy was determined through an analysis of affective objectives that was undertaken to determine the unique characteristics the affective domain should portray. The terms interest, appreciation, attitudes, values, and adjustment were obtained from this objective analysis, but the range of meanings attached to these terms were too wide to permit them to serve as the names of the classification levels. The behavioral components which were finally chosen to represent the classification level and sub-category structure were, however, at least partially a result of this objective analysis.

The affective taxonomy does, when viewed as a whole, represent a useable guideline for goal setting and objective development. There are, however, four reservations or suggestions this author will make as a means to better operationalize the taxonomy for affective objective-writing purposes. First, the receiving classification level, 1.00, is not amenable to the development of affective behavioral objectives. Receiving does not represent a level that includes an affective behavioral response, such as is found in level 2.00, Responding.

Evaluation to determine success in achieving any goal established for this classification level would depend upon cognitive, not affective, understandings and responses. Thus, it is not recommended that anyone write an affective behavioral objective at this level.

Second, a person's willingness to respond to a stimulus by one's own volition or in a manner that indicates his/her true feeling or emotion is essential in the affective domain. Esbensen[4] attested to this point when he wrote, "Perhaps the most important difference between the psychomotor and cognitive domains on the one hand, and the affective domain on the other, is the difference between can do and will do." According to this statement, the question in affective response is not whether the learner can make the desired response, which we can assume he/she can, but whether the learner is willing to make the response of his/her own accord.

For this reason, the first sub-category of the responding classification level, 2.10—Acquiescence in Responding—cannot be used to state affective behavioral objectives. Acquiescence permits a learner to acquiesce or respond as required to a given situation, command, or question. This type of compliance does not necessarily indicate any positive feeling or emotion on the learner's part. In fact, he/she may respond in a desired manner although his/her feelings and natural inclinations were opposed to the required behavior. Thus, willingness to respond, the second sub-category in the responding classification level, is the lowest sub-category that can be used for specification of objectives in behavioral terms.

Third, the fourth and fifth classification levels of the taxonomy, 4.00—Organization and 5.00—Characterization by a Value Complex, do not appear to be practical for use in normal teaching situations or with most projects at the local school level. The period of time that would be required to accomplish change at these higher levels and the inability of most educators or teachers to control the many variables that influence the learner, in addition to his/her classroom experiences, could prevent evaluation of success in achieving goals at these levels. In addition, few cause and effect relationships can be established to determine change in learner behavior through exposure to a particular teacher, program, or contextual situation.

Values and adjustments occur over the lifetime of a learner, not in a six-week or even one-year period of time. Teachers may help learners develop interests, appreciations, and even aid in the formulation of positive attitudes, whatever they really are; but developing and evaluating any higher levels of behavior in the affective domain are not feasible undertakings for most educators. The process for developing objectives at these higher classification levels would be the same, but the author recommends these attempts be limited to research and development teams which include personnel with considerable expertise in psychology, learning theory, and techniques of evaluation.

Finally, after excluding classification levels 1.00, 4.00, and 5.00, as well as sub-category 2.10, from those levels at which we would recommend affective behavioral objectives be stated, the author proposes to operationalize the terms interest, appreciation, attitudes, and values by limiting the interpretation of their meanings. This can be accomplished by simply referring to them by the approximate mid-points of their range of meanings, rather than by the entire range of meanings to which they have been associated in the taxonomy.

These conversions permit us to further operationalize the definitions of these terms to include the following:

1. Interest — a perceptual condition combining both cognitive and affective consciousness into a type of feeling which represents a willingness to respond to specific stimuli.

2. Appreciation — emotional awareness of the significance of something that is indicative of a person's potential to receive satisfaction in responding to specific stimuli.

3. Attitudes — emotionalized dispositions utilized in the information processing aspects of behavior which will cause a person to think or behave either positively or negatively toward a particular variable. Positive behavior would include the acceptance, preference, or commitment of a learner toward specific stimuli.

4. Values — any quality or trait deemed worthy enough to be desirable as indicated by a person's acceptance, preference, or commitment to specific stimuli.

The reason for operationally defining these four terms can be readily ascertained by reference to Figure 10.1. None of the terms defined now have a range of meaning covering three different classification levels. Interest and appreciation now represent only one sub-category classification each. Attitudes and values are now both defined to represent any one of the three sub-categories of the valuing classification.

Thus, these two terms may be utilized interchangeably in identifying the three sub-categories of valuing. Figure 10.1 also identifies the responding and valuing classification levels as the only levels of the taxonomy recommended by the author as appropriate for most educators to use as a basis for behavioral objective writing.

Figure 10.1. Relationships between the affective taxonomy and the meanings of four specifically defined affective terms.

TAXONOMY CLASSIFICATION LEVEL	SUB-CATEGORY CLASSIFICATION LEVEL	DEFINED AFFECTIVE TERMS
2.0 Responding	2.2—Willingness to Respond 2.3—Satisfaction in Response	Interest Appreciation
3.0 Valuing	3.1—Acceptance of Value 3.2—Preference for Value 3.3—Commitment	Attitudes and Values

Relationships Between the Affective Taxonomy and the Competency Development Theory

The competency development theory was presented in Chapter III. This theory indicates that learning will occur through a process in which stimuli and their reinforcement cause an organism to react. Thus, all learning can be said to begin with a learner being sensitized to the existence of stimuli. Eventually, the learner becomes aware of the stimulus. This awareness, occurring at the perceptual stage in the receiving phase of learning, in turn, causes some form of feeling, such as interest or disinterest, which will sooner or later result in the individual deciding to pursue the activity or to discontinue his/her contact.

Assuming that the feeling is pleasurable and that a substantial amount of curiosity or interest occurs so that the stimulus is pursued, it may continue until appreciation, attitudes, or values have been established. In a sense, affective learning can be said to take place on a pleasure-pain continuum according to the type of feeling that is produced. Most educators will perhaps prefer to refer to the pleasure-pain continuum as being a positive-negative continuum. We may conceptualize the stimulus activity as occurring in the central portion of the continuum and that a learner's contact with stimuli will result in the possibility of producing three distinct types of feeling. We may feel: (1) pain from which we may choose to withdraw; (2) indifference; or (3) pleasure to the extent we may become attracted toward the stimuli.

It may be assumed that the further along the continuum a feeling moves toward either polar extreme and away from the central portion or point of neutrality, the greater will be the amount of either pleasure or pain (positive or negative) that is experienced. This idea along with the relationships that can be established between the responding and valuing levels of the affective taxonomy and the competency development theory can be seen graphically by reference to Figure 10.2.

Figure 10.2 shows a stimulus being picked up by a learner's pri-

Figure 10.2. Relationships between the competency development theory and the major components of the responding and valuing classification levels of the affective taxonomy.

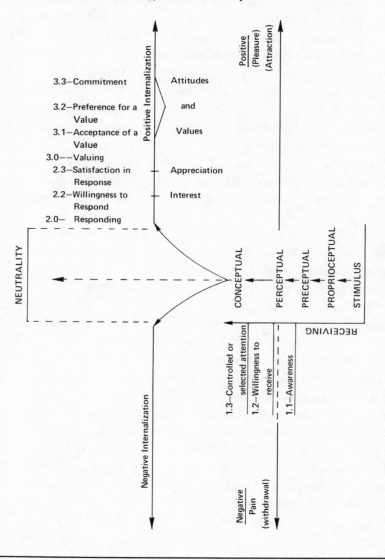

mary sensory receptors, referred to as the proprioceptual stage of learning. The stimulus is then transmitted to the preceptual stage, representing the central nervous system which interprets the stimulus and gives further instructions. From the preceptual stage, the stimulus is passed on to the perceptual stage, where a mental image of the stimulus is formed and general awareness occurs. Following a learner's awareness, the stimulus is passed on immediately to the conceptual learning stage, which results in thought formulation.

The first classification level of the affective taxonomy, receiving, may be considered to be started by initiation of stimuli in the proprioceptual stage and to end at the point of conceptualization. As soon as the learner becomes aware of a stimulus, which can be thought of as occurring at a point of neutrality on the positive-negative continuum, he/she may tend to develop either a positive or negative reaction toward it. How positive or how negative the feeling becomes may be referred to as the degree of negative or positive internalization. Obviously, some stimuli will be such that the learner may remain indifferent toward them and, in that event, the feeling will remain in the area defined as neutrality.

Assuming that a stimulus brings pleasure to the learner and that he/she becomes somewhat attracted toward it, positive internalization that occurs in the learner is what differentiates the sub-categories in classification levels 2.00, Responding, and 3.00, Valuing. Figure 10.1 reveals that interest and appreciation represent levels 2.20 and 2.30, respectively, and that attitudes and values have been operationally defined to be used interchangeably to represent sub-categories 3.10, 3.20, and 3.30.

Goal Setting and Evaluation

The technique for writing affective objectives is no different from that used to write objectives in the cognitive and psycho-motor domains. First, the educator must perform his/her goal setting activities to determine the affective competency to be achieved. Second, the objective developer must determine what type of a behavioral outcome would be most appropriate for use in evaluating learner success in achieving the desired competency.

The use of the affective taxonomy provides a good and reasonable guide for establishing goal statements. Since the primary considerations are the identification of the content, represented by stimuli, and the degree of positive internalization that is expected, the objective developer can simply incorporate the wording of the sub-category levels 2.20 through 3.30 into the goal statement, or substitute the appropriate terms interest, appreciation, attitudes, and values. These components are worded to include the learner or learner group and content in a manner that will communicate effectively the learning outcomes that are to be the intent or purpose of the objective.

There are many data collection techniques that can be useful in providing measurement data useful in the evaluation of learner success in achieving affective goals. Valid information for evaluation purposes can be either objective or subjective. The primary considerations will be to be able to ascertain that the learner's performance is congruent with the degree of internalization identified in the goal and that the learner chooses the response according to his/her own volition as evidence of his/her true feelings. Among the data collection techniques recommended for use are the following:

A. *Personal Observations.* Direct observations and interviews fall under this category. In direct observations, an educator will observe a sample of a learner's behavior to determine if a specific feeling or emotion is present and to what degree. All observations should be as factual and quantitative as possible.

Interviews usually consist of oral questions submitted to students in such a manner that they feel free to make any response they desire. Interviews provide the advantage of face-to-face contact that is lost by most survey techniques. Interviewers may obtain confidential information and both the interviewer and learner can make their own value judgments through this type of personal interaction. The interviewer should be aware of the fact that a learner may only provide the information that he/she thinks the interviewer wants to hear.

The criteria for indicating feeling under the personal observation techniques will include the learner's:

(1) desire to talk about something;

(2) desire to acquire or purchase an object;

(3) desire to involve others in some activity;

(4) desire to write about a specific topic; and

(5) desire to continue or further the relationship with something.

B. *Rating Scales.* Rating scales include the recording of information concerning a learner's stated interests, appreciations, attitudes, values, or other feelings and emotions. These scales differ from cognitive testing in that they have no correct or incorrect answers.

Rating scales should primarily consist of behavioral responses which are relevant to the particular variables being studied and should furnish hard data of an objective quantitative nature. Educators appear to prefer rating scales over the use of interviews and surveys for the evaluation of highly internalized feelings such as attitudes, values, and motivations. The most widely used types of rating scales appear to be the Likert and the semantic-differential devices for measuring the strengths of learner-stated attitudes.

C. *Surveys.* Most surveys are based upon the asking of direct questions to determine the opinions of both individuals and groups. The survey instruments usually attempt to determine a learner's positive-negative reactions concerning specific variables or to determine his/her likes or dislikes (approval or disapproval) of various stimuli.

D. *Additional Data Gathering Techniques.* Consideration may be given to the use of devices such as: (1) checklists; (2) charts;

(3) graphs; (4) sociograms; (5) anecdotal records; and (6) various projective techniques. In addition, data can be gathered by instruments designed to present statements which allow the learner to make a simple choice of either yes or no to indicate his/her positive or negative agreement with the concept presented.

Writing Behavioral Objectives
Using the Affective Taxonomy

The elimination of eight sub-category classifications from the taxonomy greatly reduces the teacher's task in developing affective objectives. It may, however, tend to insure that objectives written for the remaining sub-categories are better understood and perhaps evaluated more efficiently. The objective-writing emphasis for the remaining portion of this chapter will be focused upon the following classification levels and their sub-categories:

2.00 Responding
    2.20 Willingness to Respond;
    2.30 Satisfaction in Response;
3.00 Valuing
    3.10 Acceptance of a Value
    3.20 Preference for a Value
    3.30 Commitment

2.00—Responding

Behavioral objectives written for sub-categories of this classification level assume that learners have already been sensitized to the learning content in question or that this will be accomplished prior to the learner being required to exhibit a measurable behavioral outcome. In other words, the learners will have received the initial stimulus and will have become aware of something that has not alienated them to the point they would choose to avoid it, and that enough positive internalization of the object has taken place that they will focus their attention upon it as an act of personal satisfaction.

2.20 *Willingness to Respond*

English 101 students who are deficient in writing skills should develop an interest in seeking individual help, so that when given a written analysis of the skills that need improvement and a time schedule indicating when help is available to them, they will voluntarily seek out the instructor, special tutor, or laboratory session designed to provide them with individual help at least once a week for six weeks.

or

English 101 students who are deficient in writing skills should acquire a willingness to seek individual help, so that when given a written analysis of the skills that need improvement and a time schedule indicating when help is available to them, they will voluntarily seek out the instructor, special tutor, or laboratory session designed to provide them with individual help at least once a week for six weeks.

Critique:
  I. Goal
      A. Learner Group—English 101 students who are deficient in writing skills
      B. Learning Task—
          (1) Content—seeking individual help to improve writing skills
          (2) Domain—Affective 2.20 level (both the terms interest and willingness indicate the second sub-category of this classification level)
          (3) Future Time Orientation—should develop and should acquire
  II. Behavioral Outcome (Evaluation)
      A. Performance—to seek out the instructor, special tutor, or laboratory session
      B. Criterion Standard—to demonstrate the performance voluntarily and at least once a week for six weeks
      C. Optional Statement—so that when given a written analysis of the skills that need improvement and a time schedule indicating when help is available to them

Additional Objectives Without Critique

1. Mrs. Smith's class of kindergarten students will become willing to act out parts in dramatizations of fairy tales, so that when given the opportunity to listen to the teacher read fairy tales at story hour for one month and the opportunity to participate, each child will volunteer for at least one role in one of the three stories chosen to be acted out.

2. Eighth grade typing students will develop an interest in increasing their typing accuracy as evidenced by an increase of at least ten percent in the number of students who voluntarily come each day for the last two weeks of the semester to type during their free homeroom time.

3. Third grade students will acquire an interest in reading as evidenced by their performing at least two of the following four activities:

    (1) voluntarily using free time in the reading corner;

    (2) without teacher suggestion, reading to classmates;

    (3) asking for permission to check books out of the library; or

    (4) bring books into class to share with classmates.

2.30 Satisfaction in Response

Freshman students at Florida Junior College will develop an appreciation for the use of field trips in studying their natural environment. Given three nature hikes on which they observe their physical surroundings (trees, flowers, birds, insects, rocks, stars, physical processes, and the like), the majority of the students will, when questioned, voice approval and commend the use of the field trips as a basis for developing keen enjoyment of nature.

or

Freshman students at Florida Junior College will acquire satisfaction in using field trips to study their natural environment. Given three nature hikes on which they observe their physical surroundings (trees, flowers, birds, insects, rocks, stars, physical processes, and the like), the majority of the students will, when questioned, voice approval and commend the use of field trips as a basis for developing keen enjoyment of nature.

Critique:

I. Goal

    A. Learner Group—Freshman students at Florida Junior College

    B. Learning Task—

        (1) Content—the use of field trips in studying natural environment

        (2) Domain—Affective at 2.30 level (both appreciation and satisfaction indicate this level)

        (3) Future Time Orientation—will develop and will acquire

II. Behavioral Outcome (Evaluation)

    A. Performance—oral response

    B. Criterion Standard—the majority will voice approval and commend the use of field trips

    C. Optional Statement—given three nature hikes on which ... and the like

Additional Objectives Without Critique

1. Seventh grade science students will increase their satisfaction in utilizing performance contracts as part of their instructional resource material. Proof this goal is attained will be evidenced by 70 percent of the students scoring at least 25 percent fewer negative responses on a 30-item rating scale administered before and after the use of performance contracts in two of their units of study.

2. Ninth grade humanities students will develop an appreciation of Han-

del's Oratorio, "The Messiah." Success will be determined by their increased expression of satisfaction as evidenced by their desire:

(1) to listen to the work,

(2) to discuss the merits of the work, and

(3) to share the work with their friends.

3. Ninth grade drama students should learn to gain satisfaction from role-playing, so that when given the opportunity, at least 25 percent of the students will, of their own accord, improvise skits for presentation at school assemblies.

There are many action words that may be used to help clarify the level of internalization of performance at the responding level. These terms include willingness, willful, be sensitive to, volunteer, deliberately, commend, enjoy, approve, augment, applaud, satisfaction, etc.

3.00—Valuing

To qualify for the valuing classification level, the learner must have internalized his/her feelings to the point that the stimulus or object of concern is felt to have substantial worth and that attitudes and values are being developed. Valuing is the most widely used classification level by most educational practitioners, but, frequently, the term attitude is misused or not well defined and the desired competency might well be better identified as an interest or appreciation. Accuracy in defining the desired competency can pay large dividends when one attempts to evaluate success in achieving it.

There appear to be few "ideal" attitudes, since they are generally based upon values that are inconsistently held by the whole of society. For this reason, the norm representing the feelings held by a learner's society or community, in general, may be safer or more desirable than an attitude based upon the judgment of a single individual. This is of no concern to the teacher who is trying to individualize his/her instruction, but can be important in formulating goals and objectives for large groups of students.

At this classification level, the competency or goal statement will usually include the terms "attitudes," "values," or wording from the sub-category classification levels, such as acceptance, preference, and commitment.

3.10 Acceptance of a Value

Duval County teachers should learn to accept the value of teacher education centers, so that when they are given a semantic-differential attitude scale, composed of 20 concepts about which they are expected to be concerned and scaled from –3 to +3, 70 percent of the teachers will achieve at least a +1 rating for 17 of the concepts.

or

Duval County teachers should develop positive attitudes toward teacher education centers, so that when they are given a semantic-differential attitude scale, composed of 20 concepts about which they are expected to be concerned and scaled from –3 to +3, 70 percent of the teachers will achieve at least a +1 rating for 17 of the concepts.

Critique:
I. Goal
   A. Learner Group—Duval County teachers
   B. Learning Task—
      (1) Content—teacher education centers
      (2) Domain—Affective at 3.10 level (the terms accept the value and attitudes indicate this level)
      (3) Future Time Orientation—should learn and should develop
II. Behavioral Outcome (Evaluation)
   A. Performance—writing answers on a rating scale
   B. Criterion Standard—at least a +1 rating on 17 of 20 concepts
   C. Optional Statement—so that when they are given ... from –3 to +3

Additional Objectives Without Critique

1. Fourth grade students will accept the value of good citizenship behavior so that when given a 15-item rating scale related to the citizenship expectancy of their peer group, they will scale at least 12 of the identified behavior patterns of good citizenship positively.

2. Fifth grade students should develop an acceptance of the value of having respect for their classmates' personal belongings. Success will be evidenced by students doing at least one of the following:
   (1) the majority of the students helping keep the classroom orderly;
   (2) students consciously seeking the rightful owner of misplaced items; or
   (3) a decrease in the number of thefts reported by the same students during their sixth year at school.

3.20 Preference for a Value

Sixth grade music students will develop a preference for musical values and insights as a source of leisure time activity as determined by a teacher survey of their leisure time hobbies at home on which it is determined that 50 percent of the students frequently seek out at least two of the following stated activities:

(1) to develop their creative and expressive nature through music;
(2) to find satisfaction and meaning in music experience;
(3) to develop skills to express their emotions through music;
(4) to exercise good music judgment;
(5) to be sensitive to music; or
(6) to increase their understanding of the world and its cultures (with emphasis on their own) through an understanding of the expressive elements of music and their interaction with elements of society.

Critique:
I. Goal
   A. Learner Group—Sixth grade music students
   B. Learning Task—
      (1) Content—musical values and insights as a source of leisure time activity
      (2) Domain—Affective at 3.20 level (preference for values establishes this level)
      (3) Future Time Orientation—will develop
II. Behavioral Outcome (Evaluation)
   A. Performance—participation in selective activities
   B. Criterion Standard—seeking out at least two of the selected activities
   C. Optional Statement—none

Additional Objectives Without Critique

1. John Jones should acquire a preference for reading, so that when given a choice of quiet classroom activities such as reading, games, and art projects, etc., he will choose reading at least three out of five times.

2. Terry Parker Band students will develop a preference for "good music" for their own personal listening enjoyment, as evidenced by at least one-half of the students checking out an increased number of "good music" recordings from the music library during the second semester of school.

3.30 Commitment

Parents of ICS and IAS participants, should acquire commitment to aid their children's progress in school as measured by two-thirds of the parents becoming actively involved in at least two of the following activities:

(1) attend PAC meetings at the school level and become acquainted with the total school program;

(2) attend PAC meetings at the district level and become knowledge-able of the Title I offerings and compare with those in their school;

(3) offer their services to their child's school as a volunteer aide;

(4) encourage other parents to assist in the school and PAC meetings;

(5) offer their support and make suggestions to the teachers and the principal, etc.; or

(6) other equivalent activities which show strong feeling or obligation.

Critique:

I. Goal

A. Learner Group—Parents of ICS and IAS participants

B. Learning Task—

(1) Content—to aid their children's progress in school

(2) Domain—Affective at 3.30 level (commitment is indicator of 3.30)

(3) Future Time Orientation—should acquire

II. Behavioral Outcome (Evaluation)

A. Performance—involvement in specifically stated activities

B. Criterion Standard—active involvement in at least two of the se-lected activities

C. Optional Statement—none

Additional Objectives Without Critique

1. The ninth grade physical education students should acquire commit-ment to appropriate social, mental, or physical problems that affect their own community populace. Success can be measured by over 50 percent of the ninth graders seeking out opportunities for personal involvement in at least one or more of the following activities:

(1) participating in a physical education summer enrichment program;

(2) organizing a community athletic club;

(3) writing a letter stating needs for available community playground equipment;

(4) attending any of the in-service meetings offered in physical educa-tion activities; or

(5) taking part on a committee organized to study the community problems in depth; to a better understanding of all phases of the issues involved.

2. Eleventh grade science students should acquire commitment to current ecological problems that affect their own community as measured by 60 per-cent of the students seeking out opportunities for active involvement in at least one ecological project.

3. Fifth grade students will develop a positive attitude toward their own school's *Pitch In and Keep America Beautiful Program*. Success will be evi-denced by their commitment to the active support of at least one aspect of the program, such as regular involvement in:

(1) collecting aluminum cans and other aluminum articles for recycling;
(2) collecting paper and other trash from the school grounds and placing it in the proper receptacles for disposal; or
(3) keeping the rooms and the halls of the school clean by not throwing paper or trash on the floor, and picking up such trash when they see it.

In summing up the valuing classification level, we find that sub-category 3.10 refers to the acceptance of the worth of an idea, object, or behavior. Attitudes or values at this level become associated with the beliefs held by the individual, but are not established firmly enough to have become set or fixed.

Sub-category 3.20 occurs when feeling has not only developed to the acceptance stage, but has further been internalized to the point that one value is placed higher or considered to be more important than another. This is evidenced by a person's willingness to seek out an idea, object, or behavior in order to become involved with it.

Commitment, sub-category 3.30, means that the internalization of a feeling or emotion has reached the stage that a person feels obligated to show faith, trust, confidence, obligation for, loyalty to, or will pledge to do something. The more commitment the learner has for something, the more he/she may be expected to promote it or to become involved in it. The more the learner promotes something, the higher he/she is likely to value it.

Action terms, such as be loyal to, see value in, defend, prefer, favor, accept, seek out, show commitment to, feel strongly about, argue, support, obligate, pledge, show faith in, trust, and confidence, are all useful indicators for the valuing classification level. Usually, a learner may exhibit behavior at each of the sub-category levels as he/she proceeds to the commitment stage. He/she may first show acceptance, then indicate a preference for some value over other values he/she accepts, and eventually make some attempt to sell, convince, or change someone else's viewpoint concerning the value. Eventually, the learner may become so committed that his/her promotion of a value may take on the characteristics of a compelling impulse to act in relationship to the value.

Finally, the .author would like to give further credit to an unidentified group of teachers and administrators in the University of North Florida service area. These educators, representing former students, have from time to time submitted objectives of various types to the author as evidence of the usefulness and continuing value they have received in using objectives in their own content areas of reference. As was the case in the cognitive and psychomotor domains, all of the affective objectives used as examples in this chapter were developed and implemented to meet a particular need of some teachers and a group of students. It is important that sample illustrations be practical in real-life situations if the reader is to benefit substantially from them.

Notes

1. David R. Krathwohl *et al. Taxonomy of Educational Objectives: The Classification of Educational Goals: Handbook 2: Affective Domain* (New York: Longman, Inc., 1964), p. 53.
2. *Ibid.*, pp. 1-193.
3. Robert F. Mager. *Preparing Instructional Objectives* (Palo Alto, California: Fearon Publishers, 1962), p. 60.
4. Thorwald Esbensen. *Using Performance Objectives.* Published by the State of Florida, Department of Education in Cooperation with the Bureau of Educational Personnel Development, U.S. Office of Education, Office of Publications and Textbook Services, Knott Building, Tallahassee, Florida, p. 29.

XI.

Writing Non-Learning Oriented Performance Objectives: Accountability Through Systems Analysis and MBO

"No matter how lofty you are in your department, the responsibility for what your lowliest assistant is doing is yours."
—Bessie R. Jones and Mary Waterstreet

"I had six honest serving men: their names were Where and What and When and Why and How and Who."
—Rudyard Kipling

CHAPTER GOALS

The reader should:

1. acquire comprehension of the systems analysis and Management By Objectives techniques for establishing accountability;
2. develop skill in writing non-learning oriented performance objectives.

In Chapter III, non-learning oriented objectives were mentioned briefly as another type of performance objective that can be used to establish accountability for programs which are work rather than content oriented. In these job related areas, accountability is generally established by goal setting, and frequently accomplished through Management By Objectives (MBO), systems analysis, or task analysis. The significant point in establishing program accountability through the use of non-learning oriented performance objectives is that the emphasis is never on content or domain, but upon successfully assuming various types of job responsibilities. In other words, "educating students" is replaced by emphasis upon the *performance of specific tasks related to one's employment.*

Accountability implies: (1) someone assumes responsibility; (2) he/she is accountable to someone else; and (3) there will be an evaluation performed to determine whether or not the accountable person achieves success. The processes involved in establishing accountability are:

1. Goals are set which clearly delineate who is assuming responsibility.
2. Goals are converted to performance objectives, which are stated in measurable terms.
3. The line of authority is clearly established.
4. The conditions under which the responsibility is to be carried out are clearly specified, provided they are anything other than normal or are not self-evident.
5. Work assignments are performed and evaluated to determine the success of the accountable person.

These processes reveal that there is little difference between the processes used for establishing content accountability for students, utilizing behavioral objectives, and the processes for establishing performance task accountability in business, industry, and management through the use of non-learning oriented objectives. In education, students are accountable for a learning outcome, whereas management requires their employees to be accountable for work assignments.

Management By Objectives (MBO)

The key to MBO, a parent process to the behavioral objective movement, is goal setting. In fact, goal setting is the very heart of any program involving accountability; thus, it becomes the heart of all performance objective development, including both learning oriented and non-learning oriented objectives. Under the MBO concept of accountability, goal setting should begin with top management and then filter down to include all other employees.

Within the framework of most organizations or institutions are global mission goals or other major goals of a rather broad nature for which the top administrator must assume responsibility. These goals, sometimes set by a board of directors, establish the basis for the top administrator's accountability. Once the major goals of a top administrator are established, he/she will assist his/her top level assistant administrators in establishing their goals, which must be consistent with the needs established by his/her own goals and within any constraints which they may impose.

Next, the top level assistant administrators will meet with their own subordinate administrators in order to help them select the goals for which they and their subordinates will become accountable. The subordinate administrators meet, in turn, with *their* subordinates to aid in setting goals.

This process is repeated in chainlike fashion from the top administrator down through all levels of subordinate administrators and other employees until goals have been established for all of an organization's or institution's personnel. Goal setting of this nature has a ripple-like effect insofar as one broad goal or mission at the top administrator level may result in hundreds of goals being established throughout the entire organization.

A primary concept to remember in applying MBO is that goals are not arbitrarily established and assigned by those in authority. The entire process requires that goals be established cooperatively, insofar as possible and practical, by the person who will perform the function and the person to whom he/she is accountable. Eventually, each goal that is set must be analyzed to determine what evidence will be acceptable to determine employee success in meeting his/her responsibility. Thus, the concept of employee evaluation is introduced as a means of verifying accountability. This requires that any goal which is important enough to be identified in goal setting should be restated as a performance objective.

Systems Analysis

Systems analysis is primarily a process for determining what needs to be done in order to achieve a desired mission or to solve a specifically identified problem. Practically speaking, *systems analysis is a process for analyzing and presenting a mission (problem) in a reasonably logical and understandable pattern so that whatever needs to be done to solve the problem can be identified, executed, and controlled efficiently.* This process attempts to determine every function, activity, and task that needs to be done to solve a given mission or problem. In addition, systems analysis is concerned with when each activity or task will be implemented and who will be accountable for its success.

Systems analysis may be performed by a special team of program planners or by management itself. The systems which result from systems analysis are generally referred to as performance systems. This type of system receives its name from its emphasis upon determining accountability through goal setting and the development of performance objectives.

Systems analysis is not the same thing as MBO, but can be used along with MBO and results in the same type of employee accountability. Again, systems analysis is work oriented rather than content oriented, although it functions much the same as did the systematic competency analysis technique outlined in Chapter VI of this text.

As was the case in MBO, systems are developed as a process approach to accountability. Performance objectives are used throughout every phase and stage of performance system development. All components of a performance system have target goals stated as performance objectives. This focuses the assignment of work tasks upon activities that are important to the successful implementation and evaluation of the system.

Both MBO and systems analysis planning enable administrators to better manage their human and material resources to meet present and future needs. Both of these accountability techniques result in the development of the non-learning oriented type of performance objectives. In essence, each of these two techniques establishes comparable programs of accountability, but they are arrived at in a different manner.

Since the behavioral objectives movement followed on the heels of the MBO and systems analysis movements, it is obvious why many of the problems in the use and writing of behavioral objectives have occurred. One significant problem has been that many behaviorist advocates have failed to recognize or admit the difference between a learning task that is content and domain oriented and a work task that is performance oriented. In learning tasks, it is the learning of the content that increases a learner's capabilities. It is the end, not the performance, that determines whether or not learning has occurred. Performances are considered to be only samples of many alternative performances that could be used. In work tasks, the relationship between goals to be achieved and the work task performed may be much closer, and in some instances they can even be considered to be identical.

Writing Non-Learning Oriented Performance Objectives

There is very little difference in the writing and establishing of non-learning oriented accountability and accountability involving learning oriented situations. Both require the use of performance objectives which have been defined in the "goals approach" to mean any specifically stated objective with two components, a goal and an evaluation indicator. The goal identifies the specific intent or purpose of the objective and the evaluation indicator refers to some type of performance or activity that will be utilized to determine the level of success in achieving the precisely stated goal.

Figure 11.1 clearly illustrates the two types of objectives, learning and non-learning oriented, which come under the label of performance objective. The two major components of an objective statement, the goal and evaluation, are also depicted. In addition, this figure identifies the necessary parts that the goal and evaluation components must include in order for the objective to clearly communicate all of the desired information needed to establish accountability.

This figure clearly reveals the similarities and differences between the two performance objective classifications. Both types of performance objectives are based upon specifically stated goals and evaluation indicators. Both types identify someone who will be responsible for goal achievement and the task for which he/she will be accountable. In addition, both the learning and non-learning oriented objectives require an evaluation performance and a criterion for determining success.

The primary difference between the two classifications is found in the type of a task to be achieved. The behavioral objective identifies a learning task that is content and domain oriented, whereas the non-learning oriented objective identifies a program task that is work oriented. The evaluation components are essentially the same except the performances or instrumentation used to determine success will naturally be altered by the type of goal that is being evaluated.

The Basic Goal Statement

A non-learning oriented goal, generally selected through MBO, systems analysis, needs assessment, task analysis, or some other method, should represent the specific intent of a course of action for which someone is to be held accountable. Some examples of basic non-learning oriented goal statements are:

Figure 11.1. Classification of performance objectives.

PERFORMANCE OBJECTIVE	
Non-Learning Oriented Objective	**Learning Oriented (Behavioral) Objective**

I. GOAL – Identifies
 	
a. Who
b. Work or Program task
  (1) What
  (2) When
 	
II. EVALUATION – Identifies
 	
a. Performance, activity, or documentation
 	
b. Criterion or standard for success
	I. GOAL – Identifies
	
	a. Learner
	b. Learning task
	  (1) Content
	  (2) Domain
	  (3) Future time orientation
	
	II. EVALUATION – Identifies
	
	a. Performance, behavior, instrumentation, or activity
	b. Criterion or standard for success

1. The finance committee will prepare and present by January 20, 1979, a cost analysis of the management plan for training substitute teachers.
2. The Director of Special Education will develop, by September 1, 1980, a management plan for implementing a new TMR program.
3. Teachers in the math department will design self-instructional learning packets for a complete course in intermediate algebra before the end of the school year.
4. The head librarian will provide each English instructor with a mimeographed list of all English related visual aids and materials available in the college library by September 15.
5. The reading committee will develop curriculum guidelines within 60 calendar days for the content area of reading.
6. The Director of Staff Development will develop a master plan within 30 calendar days for an in-service education program that will provide the training necessary to implement the guidelines for the reading program.
7. The philosophy committee will formulate, within 20 calendar days, statements of philosophy and rationale that will serve as guidelines for the development and improvement of the elementary reading program.
8. School media specialists will develop by the Spring of 1979, a plan for the implementation of the open library concept of media center management in each school media center in the district.
9. The county curriculum division will develop and publish by August, 1979, a program for Career Education in the secondary school.
10. Educators in St. Johns County will develop by June, 1979, a program providing an alternative educational process for disruptive children.

Checking Basic Goal Statements
for Appropriate Communication

The communication check of non-learning oriented goal statements is taken from that used in Management By Objectives (MBO). The checks consist of: (1) who, (2) what, and (3) when. They are interpreted as meaning who will do what program task and when must it be accomplished. Using the first four of the previously stated basic non-learning oriented goal statements, we can illustrate the technique for critiquing as follows:

1. The finance committee will prepare and present by January 20,

1979, a cost analysis of the management plan for training substitute teachers.

Critique:

A. Basic Goal Statement
  (1) Who—the finance committee
  (2) What—will prepare and present a cost analysis of the management plan for training substitute teachers
  (3) When—by January 20, 1979

2. The Director of Special Education will develop, by September 1, 1980, a management plan for implementing a new TMR program.

Critique:

A. Basic Goal Statement
  (1) Who—the Director of Special Education
  (2) What—will develop a management plan for implementing a new TMR program
  (3) When—by September 1, 1980

3. Teachers in the math department will design self-instructional learning packets for a complete course in intermediate algebra before the end of the school year.

Critique:

A. Basic Goal Statement
  (1) Who—teachers in the math department
  (2) What—will design self-instructional learning packets for a complete course in intermediate algebra
  (3) When—before the end of the school year

4. The head librarian will provide each English instructor with a mimeographed list of all English related visual aids and materials available in the college library by September 15.

Critique:

A. Basic Goal Statement
  (1) Who—the head librarian
  (2) What—will provide each English instructor with a mimeographed list of all English related visual aids and materials available in the college library
  (3) When—by September 15

These four goal statements can be considered to be adequate since each one identifies: (1) the person or group who is accountable; (2) the program or work task for which they are responsible; and (3) the date or time allotment that will be allowed for the completion of each assignment.

Converting Basic Goal Statements
to Performance Objectives

The non-learning oriented goals previously stated will serve as the basis for illustrating the development of non-learning oriented performance objectives. As was the case with behavioral objectives, non-learning oriented objectives are formed by simply adding an evaluation performance and a criterion standard when appropriate. Generally speaking, performance objectives should not try to include either more or less information in the evaluation component than the requirement of the goal. In other words, they should be congruent.

There may be instances in which the complete objective may not need to include a criterion standard. This is particularly true of objectives which are at a low level of complexity. It is sufficient, at this point, to just mention this possibility. The art of writing non-learning oriented performance objectives will, however, be focused upon writing objectives that are complete in every respect.

The measurement or activity in the evaluation component may or may not be performed by the person or group who is accountable. This is a departure from the requirement of a behavioral objective in which it is only the accountable learner who can do the performance which will be evaluated to determine success in goal achievement. Each objective should have at least some evidence of a performance or documentation that something has been accomplished. In addition, as a minimum criterion requirement, some indication should be included that the work performed has been approved by some higher authority. The non-learning oriented goals previously stated will serve as the basis for illustrating the development of non-learning oriented performance objectives. The goals will be italicized so that they can be readily identified separately from each objective's evaluation component.

1. *The finance committee will prepare and present by January 20, 1979, a cost analysis of the management plan for training substitute teachers.* Success-

ful attainment of this goal will be demonstrated by a written document submitted to and approved by the Director of Finance and Accounting, which will include the following:

(a) cost of personnel
(b) cost of facilities
(c) cost of materials and resources
(d) cost of travel

2. *The Director of Special Education will develop, by September 1, 1980, a management plan for implementing a new TMR program.* Success will be evidenced by a completed written document which details the following:

(a) a philosophy and rationale
(b) a summary of findings from existing programs in other areas and the recommendations made as a result of these findings
(c) an identification of state standards for TMR complete with a listing of alternative learning activities, facilities, and equipment
(d) an identification of areas of cost to the District School System
(e) an identification of specific training activities for all personnel to be involved
(f) a plan for evaluation of the TMR program
(g) a plan for revising and improving the program as the evaluation data indicates improvement is necessary

3. *Teachers in the math department will design self-instructional learning packets for a complete course in intermediate algebra before the end of the school year.* Success will be measured by learning modules complete with pre-tests, behavioral objectives, alternate learning strategies, and post-tests for each learning task in algebra being submitted to the Chairman of the Math Department by the end of the contract period and, subsequently, being approved as being ready for distribution and use.

4. *The head librarian will provide each English instructor with a mimeographed list of all English related visual aids and materials available in the college library by September 15.* Proof this goal is attained will be furnished by a checklist upon which all English teachers have recorded the date they have received the list of visual aids and materials.

5. *The reading committee will develop curriculum guidelines within 60 calendar days for the content area of reading.* Success will be achieved when a written document is submitted to and approved by the Director of Elementary Education as meeting each of the following criteria:

1. All basic skills have been identified and stated as goals.
2. Goals are placed in sequential order.
3. Each goal is converted to a performance objective.
4. Written curriculum guidelines are ready for field testing.

6. *The Director of Staff Development will develop a master plan within 30 calendar days for an in-service education program that will provide the*

training necessary to implement the guidelines for the reading program. Success will be evidenced by the completion of a written plan that is completed on time with:

(1) all training activities scheduled and locations identified;
(2) consultants selected and approved;
(3) provisions made for teacher-released time;
(4) all necessary materials selected and ordered;
(5) preparations completed for distribution of announcement notices; and
(6) approval of the Assistant Superintendent for Instruction.

7. *The philosophy committee will formulate, within 20 calendar days, statements of philosophy and rationale that will serve as guidelines for the development and improvement of the elementary reading program*. Success will be evidenced by completed, typed copies of the program philosophy and rationale that have received approval from the administrative staff and have been distributed to each organized project group on time.

8. *School media specialists will develop by the Spring of 1979, a plan for the implementation of the open library concept of media center management in each school media center in the district*. Success will be determined when the completed plan has been submitted to the Director of Instruction and approved for implementation in the schools.

9. *The county curriculum division will develop and publish by August, 1979, a program for Career Education in the secondary school*. Success in achieving this goal will be evidenced by a written comprehensive plan that outlines the program requirements and is approved by the Associate Superintendent of Instruction.

10. *Educators in St. Johns County will develop by June, 1979, a program providing an alternative educational process for disruptive children*. Success will be determined by the School Board approval of a written comprehensive plan for an alternative educational program and subsequent funding of the program.

Non-Learning Oriented Objective Critiques

Again, it is emphasized that the only person likely to critique an objective is the person who is writing it. This self-checking device is instrumental in aiding the objective writer to improve his/her proficiency in communicating essential information to the person or persons who will be held accountable for achieving the objective. Since the goal statements are italicized and have already been critiqued earlier in this chapter, we will critique only the evaluation component of four of the previously stated objectives.

1. *The reading committee will develop curriculum guidelines within 60 calendar days for the content area of reading.* Success will be achieved when a written document is submitted to and approved by the Director of Elementary Education as meeting each of the following criteria:

    1. All basic skills have been identified and stated as goals.
    2. Goals are placed in sequential order.
    3. Each goal is converted to a performance objective.
    4. Written curriculum guidelines are ready for field testing.

Evaluation Critique:

    A. Performance—a written document is developed and submitted to the Director of Elementary Education
    B. Criterion—a written document is approved by the Director of Elementary Education as having met four specifically stated criteria

2. *The Director of Staff Development will develop a master plan within 30 calendar days for an in-service education program that will provide the training necessary to implement the guidelines for the reading program.* Success will be evidenced by the completion of a written plan that is completed on time with:

    (1) all training activities scheduled and locations identified;
    (2) consultants selected and approved;
    (3) provisions made for teacher-released time;
    (4) all necessary materials selected and ordered;
    (5) preparations completed for distribution of announcement notices; and
    (6) approval of the Assistant Superintendent for Instruction.

Evaluation Critique:

    A. Performance—a written plan is developed and submitted to the Assistant Superintendent for Instruction
    B. Criterion—the written plan is completed on time and approved by the Assistant Superintendent for Instruction as having met six specific requirements or stated criteria

3. *The philosophy committee will formulate, within 20 calendar days, statements of philosophy and rationale that will serve as guidelines for the development and improvement of the elementary reading program.* Success will be evidenced by completed, typed copies of the program philosophy and rationale that have received approval from the administrative staff and have been distributed to each organized project group on time.

Evaluation Critique:

    A. Performance—typed copies of program philosophy and rationale are prepared and submitted to the administrative staff to whom the philosophy committee is accountable

      B. Criterion—in this instance, success is determined by simple approval from the administrative staff and subsequent distribution of the philosophy and rationale statements that were developed

    4. *The head librarian will provide each English instructor with a mimeographed list of all English related visual aids and materials available in the college library by September 15.* Proof this goal is attained will be furnished by a checklist upon which all English teachers have recorded the date they have received the list of visual aids and materials.

Evaluation Critique:

    A. Performance—a checklist that is prepared and used to gather data

    B. Criterion—all teachers (100%) must indicate the date they received the list of visual aids and materials

The author again wishes to express his appreciation to the teachers and administrators in the University of North Florida service area for contributing an ample supply of non-learning oriented objectives for use in this text. The ten objectives selected for use as illustrations in this chapter were chosen as being typical of the types of objectives used in various schools and in school district central offices.

Many non-learning oriented objectives require rather complex objective statements including complex evaluation indicators to determine success. Sample objective number four, however, emphasizes the fact that an objective may be quite simple. In this instance, a person (head librarian) was given a task to perform and success was determined by a checklist that would give evidence that the task either was or was not completed. The only criterion necessary was for *all* persons to date the checklist in order for the accountable person's responsibility to be resolved.

The reader should realize that the nature of the area of responsibility and the particular work to be performed will dictate what intents and evaluation indicators will be useful in writing a non-learning oriented objective. In the areas of automobile production, refrigerator manufacture, airline operation, politics, etc., the intents and evaluation indicators may be quite different from the ones used in the sample illustrations in this chapter. The technique and format for writing the objectives would, however, remain the same.

This chapter has presented the use of non-learning oriented objectives as a means for establishing employee accountability for satisfactory completion of work assignments. All accountability was shown to be based upon first identifying appropriate goals. The MBO and systems analysis techniques were shown to be two of the most useful methods of goal setting to determine work responsibilities.

The major thrust of the chapter was to develop skill in writing non-learning oriented performance objectives. The "goals approach" objective-writing technique was used as the best means to communicate both an employee's work intent and how he/she will be evaluated to determine success in achieving his/her responsibilities.

Appendix:
Sample Course Module

UNIVERSITY OF NORTH FLORIDA
COLLEGE OF EDUCATION
Department of Educational Administration and Supervision

COURSE TITLE: Systems Development:
Educational Accounta-
bility

COURSE NUMBER: EDA 605

PREREQUISITES: EDA 604 or EDA 611,
or Permission of
Professor

STUDENT INFORMATION:

NAME:

ADDRESS:

PHONE:

PRICE:

(Fall, 1977)

235

TABLE OF CONTENTS

1.00 Mission Statement

Students completing this module should acquire the competencies necessary to: (1) apply a systems approach to problem-solving, (2) develop comprehensive plans for implementing and evaluating educational programs, and (3) improve their ability to function effectively as either a teacher or administrator in a school-based management system. Success in achieving this mission will be evidenced by the achievement of each of the seven specific competencies outlined in this module at the minimum level stated or better.

1.10 Operational Definitions

1.1.1 *Competencies*—sub-goals contained within the mission statement which represent the specific learning intents to be achieved by students using the module. (Desired learning outcomes or ends.)

1.1.2 *Enabling Activities and Learning Resources*—refers to the instructional strategies and all human and material resources necessary to enable students to achieve a desired competency.

1.1.3 *Evaluation and Grade Reporting*—refers to a statement of the overall criteria that will be used in determining student achievement with reference to grades that will be forwarded to the registrar's office.

1.1.4 *Interim Objective*—represents an extension of the competency statements to include the behaviors or performances, criteria, givens, and conditions necessary for the teacher to determine student success in competency achievement.

1.1.5 *Post-Assessment Statements*—statements used to further clarify an objective by providing supplemental information. These statements are particularly useful in helping communicate more fully the behavioral outcomes outlined in the interim objectives.

1.20 Introduction

At the present time, there is a growing need at both the local and national levels to establish accountability for instructional programs as well as for many non-learning oriented activities. As is the case in all school systems, individual schools within a school system may differ widely in the quality of their instructional programs, competence of instructional personnel, and in the quality of special projects as well as all other planned activities. Thus, it becomes extremely important at times to determine what a teacher or administrator should be held accountable for and to what extent he or she can influence desired changes.

In recent years, considerable emphasis has been placed on the improvement of educational evaluation and the relating of program strategies to objectives. Currently, there is considerable focus upon systems analysis and the statement of objectives in performance terms. Improvement of educational quality is the basic goal of each of these professional endeavors. Despite this common goal, too little coordination of techniques and processes has been accomplished. Curriculum development, implementation of special projects, and learning and non-learning oriented evaluation are all important processes; but they are too frequently approached as though they are unrelated components of an educational program.

In 1971, Governor Reubin Askew appointed a special education committee to study and make recommendations for improving schools. This committee recommended that the best manner to handle the complexity of managing, teaching, and financing schools is through the establishment of school-based management systems.

The 1972 Florida Legislature established a requirement for school district comprehensive educational planning by the addition of Section 236.02 (9) F.S. In the fiscal year 1974-75, school systems in Florida were moving in the direction of implementing educational programs based upon the school-based management system concept. Planning, Programming, Budgeting, and Evaluation Systems (PPBES) is the structure that will be used to produce cost data for management information systems used by the State and district school boards.

This module is designed as a complete course of instruction to guide individual and group efforts in the use of the systems approach in accomplishing the intents of:

(1) Governor Askew's committee recommendations;

(2) the actions of the Florida Legislature; and

(3) other specific and general needs for more effective public school accountability.

Students will develop systems and accountability programs. Furthermore, they will learn to use PERT in solving time-scheduling problems, developing an understanding of needs assessment, and learning how to develop Planning, Programming, Budgeting, and Evaluation Systems.

1.30 Operational Instructions

This module is designed so that you can proceed step by step toward successful achievement of all the required competencies. Module components 1.10 through 1.40 are designed to introduce you to the module and instruct you on how to proceed through it. Module component 1.50 presents a separate sequential listing of all of the competencies to be achieved. Each competency is again identified under component 1.60 as an interim objective that has been arranged in the same logical and sequential order as 1.50.

Both the desired competency and suggested behavioral outcome, to be used in evaluating success in achieving the competency, are identified in each interim performance objective. Learning activities and resources, designed to enable students to achieve each competency, and supplementary post-assessment statements follow the specification of each performance objective. No diagnostic pre-assessment is required of students prior to attempting to achieve the competence required in this module.

The specific enabling strategies for learning the content requirements of this module include:

(1) an adopted text;

(2) supplementary text references;

(3) handout materials;

(4) overhead transparencies;

(5) lecture;

(6) workshop-type small-group interaction; and

(7) free-choice selections by the learner.

In order to determine student progress toward achieving the desired competencies, data will be collected at the completion of the enabling activities which accompany each objective. The primary types of data to be collected from the students include achievement on tests, performance on written assignments representing on-the-job types of program planning, and problem-solving activities.

Students may be examined on one or more of the required competencies at any time, subject to the convenience and discretion of the professor. Proof of student understanding of stated competencies will permit that student to "opt out" of those competencies that he/she has already achieved (without attending class sessions or proceeding through the prescribed enabling strategies).

Once the learner has achieved the desired behavioral outcome for any objective, he/she may move on to the next objective. The operational procedures to be followed in completing this module are:

1. Familiarize yourself with the specific competencies that represent the learning intents of the module.

2. Study and try to achieve each performance objective one at a time and preferably in sequence.

3. Evaluate competency achievement through instrumentation provided by the instructor or by the preparation of recommended project materials.

4. If post-assessment indicates you have failed to achieve an objective, you may recycle to achieve competence.
5. Repeat the process steps outlined in procedures two through four until you have achieved all objectives.

1.40 Evaluation and Grade Reporting

The mission statement and all specific interim performance objectives in this module are stated at the minimum level of competency expected of a graduate student. Your final grade in this course will be based upon the following guidelines:

A = Ten competencies achieved with at least seven competencies being achieved with honors.

B = Ten competencies achieved with six or fewer competencies being achieved with honors.

C = Eight or nine competencies achieved.

F = Seven or less competencies achieved.

I = Must be requested in advance by student with a passing grade and a bona fide reason.

NOTE: All performance objectives are stated at the minimum level. This means they are stated with an expected standard of achievement that would entitle a graduate student to a letter grade of "B." This is indicated by a check mark ($\sqrt{}$). A student attaining a competency above the minimum level, or with honors, receives a check plus mark ($\sqrt{}+$).

Seven specific performance objectives are stated in this module. Objectives number three and seven are given the weight of three and two respectively, due to their comprehensive nature and/or outside time requirements necessary to complete them. Thus, the letter grades A, B, or C are based on expectancy of ten (10), rather than seven (7) competencies.

1.50 Statement of Specific Competencies

Competencies, in the context used in this module, represent the specific learning intents that the professor believes will be most valuable for future student use.

Each competency is considered to be a specific instructional goal (or learning outcome intent) that has intrinsic value and is considered to be a long-range end worth achieving. In this module, you will be asked to:

1. Develop *comprehension* of a "Systems Model for Educational Accountability" and of appropriate criteria and techniques useful in conducting a systematic needs assessment. (2.10)*

2. Acquire *comprehension* of specific terms and related concepts important in the development and understanding of systems and in the use of the systems analysis process. (2.00)

3. Develop the *skills* necessary to apply systems analysis techniques in solving educational problems. (5.00)

4. Acquire *knowledge* of specific PERT terms and symbols and develop the ability to apply PERT techniques in solving problems concerning time-scheduling. (3.00)

5. Develop the *ability* to use PERT techniques in the construction of a functional control network. (3.00)

6. Develop the *ability* to apply strategy analysis processes to determine appropriate methods and means for implementing a management plan. (4.00)

7. Develop the *ability* to plan a PPBES type budget for a special cost center. (5.00)

1.60 Interim Objectives, Enabling Activities, and Learning Resources

In this module, interim objectives represent extensions of the

---

*Numbers in parentheses represent the suggested understanding level required by the objective according to Bloom's cognitive taxonomy.

specific goals or competencies (stated in Subsystem 1.50) to include the behavioral outcomes expected from the learner. These behavioral outcomes are specified by a performance statement indicating the behavior, activity, or instrumentation that will be used to evaluate learner progress toward achieving the goals. In addition, the behavioral outcome statement should include a criterion standard that represents the level of success required for a performance to be considered an adequate indication of competency achievement.

The outcome performance statements and success level criteria used to evaluate competency achievement and to convert goals to behavioral objectives in this module are not considered to have intrinsic value. They are used as a means for determining short-range success in competency achievement at a particular point in time.

Each performance objective is sequentially stated in the same order as that of its corresponding competency statement in Subsystem 1.50 of the module. All objectives are followed by the listing of enabling activities and learning resources that may be used to achieve the competency. In addition, supplementary post-assessment and recycling information is stated for each individual objective as a means of further clarifying the process for achieving each competency.

Students are expected to maintain a reasonable standard of written expression in all assignments turned in to the professor for evaluation of competency achievement. This means that in all written work, students are expected to express themselves clearly and correctly.

Interim Objective Number One

You should develop comprehension of a "Systems Model for Educational Accountability" and of appropriate criteria and techniques useful in conducting a systematic needs assessment. Success in achieving this competency will be determined by a written test consisting of 25 short answer, completion, and multiple-choice type questions on which you must score at least 20 correct answers.

Enabling Activities and Learning Resources
A. Classroom lecture
B. Read: Major text, chapters two and six
Kaufman, Roger A., *Educational System Planning,* chapter three
C. Free-choice activities

Post-Assessment Statement
Systems analysis is a process that is frequently used to solve specifically identified problems. Most problems are identified through either a formal or informal needs assessment. Time will not allow students in this course to actually carry out a comprehensive needs assessment. In addition, you have not yet mastered the necessary systems analysis techniques that are desired before beginning such a project. Your examination to determine your success in achieving this competency will require both the knowledge and comprehension levels of understanding. In the event you are not successful in achieving this competency, you may recycle (take another test) twice after consulting your professor. Both recycle tests will be similar to the first test in context and format.

Interim Objective Number Two
You should acquire comprehension of specific terms and related concepts important in the development and understanding of systems and the use of the systems analysis process. Success will be evidenced by an 11-item written examination (consisting of terms to be defined, completion, and true-false questions), on which you will achieve at least nine correct answers.

Enabling Activities and Learning Resources
A. Classroom lecture
B. Read: Major text, chapters one and eight
C. Small-group work sessions
D. Free-choice activities

Post-Assessment Statement
Professional educators preparing to enter an era characterized by school-based management systems should be able to develop their own systems as well as to take the leadership in helping to train their colleagues in the systems processes. This objective is intended to prepare the learner with the necessary prerequisite knowledge and comprehension that will be necessary for him/her to undertake the systems analysis problem stated in Interim Objective Number Three and to fulfill future work commitments involving systems development.

It is assumed that teachers and administrators must know how to perform systems analysis functions, but must also have a vocabulary sufficient to enable them to define and explain the processes to others. The competency examination will require students to memorize and to be able to paraphrase and translate specific terms and concepts.

Two recycles will be allowed if the competency is not achieved on the first examination. Both recycles will be similar to the first test in style, format, and content.

Interim Objective Number Three
You must develop the skills necessary to apply systems analysis techniques in solving educational problems. Success will be determined by your demonstrated ability to correctly perform systems analysis processes in the development of a management plan designed to solve a specific problem you have identified. The criteria to be used by the professor in evaluation of the management plan consists of:

(1) the adequacy of the mission, introduction, and/or rationale, and philosophy statements with regard to application toward the specific problem you have identified for solution;
(2) the appropriateness of the goal statements specifying "what needs to be done";
(3) the quality of the performance objectives used to establish accountability in converting the management plan into a "performance system." Particular emphasis will be placed upon the statement of overtly observable measures of evaluation which clearly indicate specific criteria for success;
(4) the creative relationships (or "goodness of fit") between the identified subsystems, subsystem components, interim components, tasks, and the mission of the system;
(5) the overall quality of the system produced (as evidenced by the person's or group's ability to follow all of the guideline steps for development of the system) and the creative ingenuity and functional utility displayed in developing a graphic description of the management plan; and
(6) group assessment of your individual contributions toward the development of the completed system by use of a peer-group-rating form.

Enabling Activities and Learning Resources
A. Classroom lecture
B. Read: Major text, chapters seven, eight, and nine
   Kaufman, Roger A., *Educational System Planning*, chapters four, five, and 11
C. Small-group work sessions
D. Independent small-group and individual field experiences
E. Free-choice activities

Post-Assessment Statement

Systems development is normally *a group process requiring good leadership, a variety of expertise, and concentration of thought*. Thus, student evaluation for the achievement of this competency will primarily be based upon the performance of a group rather than upon individual achievement. Each group will be composed of approximately five members who will develop a management plan designed to solve a specific problem the group has chosen. Individuals or pairs of students with specific job-related problems may develop their own systems rather than work in a larger group.

Your specific assignment will be to develop a management plan according to the following guidelines:

1. Begin with formalized mission, introduction and/or rationale, and philosophy statements.
2. Each mission must be broken down into at least as many subsystems as there are group members.
3. Each subsystem will be processed through the first three guideline steps for systematic management plan development—as described and illustrated in the class lecture. (A different subsystem *may* be developed by each group member.)
4. All subsystems will be broken down into at least two or more subsystem components, which have been processed through the same three guideline steps used in developing the subsystem.
5. All subsystem components will be broken down into at least two or more interim components which are also processed through the first three guideline steps.
6. One entire subsystem will be chosen by the group and processed through the first four guideline steps down through the task level, converting that part of the system to a performance system.
7. The entire system will then be checked for guideline step

number five and processed through guideline step number six.

A basic grade for each management plan will be established by the professor. In addition, all members of each group will be required to evaluate the other participants in the group. A peer-group-rating sheet will be furnished for this purpose. Individual student grades for this objective will be adjusted, either up or down, provided the data furnished by the peer-group-ratings indicates that this is appropriate.

This objective carries the weight of three competencies (as indicated under 1.40, Evaluation and Grade Reporting). The evaluation performance requires knowledge, comprehension, application, analysis, and synthesis levels of understanding. Thus, it is classified at the 5.00 level of the cognitive taxonomy. It can be recycled one time only.

Interim Objective Number Four

You will acquire knowledge of specific PERT terms and symbols and develop the ability to apply PERT techniques in solving problems concerning time-scheduling. Given a test that includes ten specific terms or symbols, 12 descriptive statements, and a specific problem to solve, you will be expected to achieve at least 80 percent correct answers.

Enabling Activities and Learning Resources
A. Classroom lecture
B. Read: Major text, chapter 13
C. Small-group work sessions
D. Independent study
E. Free-choice activities

Post-Assessment Statement
Once a system has been developed, but before it is imple-

mented, the time requirements for each activity should be determined and placed into some form of a functional control network. PERT is ideal for determining specific activity time requirements, as well as for planning the total time allocation for an entire comprehensively analyzed project.

The test to be administered in determining achievement of this competency is in two parts. Each part will carry the value of 80 percent of the exam. The first part will consist of matching specific PERT terms and symbols to descriptive statements which best define them. The second part will require you to solve a PERT time-scheduling problem to determine the following:

(1) average expected elapsed time for all activities;

(2) expected dates on which events will occur;

(3) latest allowable date for all events;

(4) slack time; and

(5) the critical path.

This objective requires application level understanding. A maximum of two recycles will be allowed students who are not successful in achieving this competency on the first test.

Interim Objective Number Five

You should develop the ability to use PERT techniques in the construction of a functional control network. Success will be evidenced by your ability to graphically illustrate and explain, in a written event-activity chart, the time-scheduling requirements of all subsystem component or interim component activities stated in your management plan. The success criteria to be used by the professor in evaluating these documents include the following:

(1) the proper use of a date line;

(2) the inclusion of all subsystem component or interim component level activities;

(3) the congruence between each t_e value as stated in the activity chart, and recorded over each activity in the con-

trol network as shown by the corresponding time consumed by the date line;

(4) the written event-activity chart must correctly identify all events, state what occurs in each activity, and give the correct t_e value; and

(5) the quality and general creativity exercised in developing the overall graphic description so that it communicates easily and accurately.

Enabling Activities and Learning Resources
A. Classroom discussion
B. Read: Major text, chapter 13
C. Independent study
D. Small-group work activities
E. Free-choice activities

Post-Assessment Statement
Each group will use PERT techniques in graphically developing a functional control network and prepare a written description of it based upon the management plan they have developed. Information must be complete for each subsystem at the interim component level. Subsystem components not broken down to the interim component level will be treated the same as interim components. The activity chart and graphic description should be complete, congruent, and accurate in every respect. You are to use application level understanding in demonstrating your achievement of this competency. You are permitted one recycle opportunity if you fail to achieve this competency during your first attempt.

Interim Objective Number Six
You will develop the ability to apply strategy analysis processes to determine appropriate methods and means for implementing a

management plan. Success in achieving this competency will be evidenced by a written document containing charts, tables, or other formats which adequately designate each methods-means combination obtained through strategy analysis of the management plan (created by systems analysis in Interim Objective Number Three). The criteria the professor will use to determine success are as follows:

(1) a table of contents;

(2) all activities at the interim component or task levels will be included as coded goal statements;

(3) alternative methods-means combinations that can be used to achieve each task (two or more for each activity);

(4) known advantages and/or disadvantages associated with the utilization of each alternative-strategy combination identified;

(5) the estimated cost of each alternative combination;

(6) the present resources available and the resources needed;

(7) a summary that states which alternative combinations are recommended for use and the reason for their selection; and

(8) any other unique information that might be of concern to decision-makers who will ultimately need to decide whether or not to implement the proposed system.

The professor will establish a basic grade for the project. This basic grade may either be raised or lowered by peer-group-rating forms that will be utilized to help determine individual student achievement and·contributions to the group project. Students will be limited to one recycle opportunity.

Enabling Activities and Learning Resources
A. Classroom lecture
B. Read: Major text, chapter ten
         Kaufman, Roger A., *Educational System Planning,* chapter seven

C. Small-group work activities
D. Independent field experience
E. Free-choice activities

Post-Assessment Statement

This objective is a group effort that requires analysis-level thinking and understanding in order to break down the management plan components in terms of the alternative methods-means combinations by which they can be implemented. In the achievement of this objective strategy, analysis will be performed at the task level (interim component level for subsystems not broken down to tasks and subsystems component level for activities not broken down to tasks or interim components). This objective carries the weight of two competencies, as previously stated.

Interim Objective Number Seven

You will develop the ability to plan a PPBES type budget for a special cost center. Success will be evidenced by your development of a program type budget which, according to the professor's judgment, meets at least 80 percent of the following content criteria:

(1) an adequate heading page depicting the proper program budget coding;

(2) well-stated educational specifications which include (a) a mission statement, (b) overall program sub-objectives, and (c) a description of methods and means for achieving the program objectives;

(3) a statement of all necessary supporting information, such as physical facilities, organizational structures, movement activity, and space requirements;

(4) a detailed program budget; and

(5) a summary page depicting itemized summaries of all of the budget categories used plus additional information that appears to be pertinent.

Enabling Activities and Learning Resources
A. Classroom discussion
B. Read: Major text, chapter 12
C. Small-group work sessions
D. Free-choice activities

Post-Assessment Statement

Planning, Programming, Budgeting, and Evaluation Systems enable educators to establish specific cost centers with specific goals and objectives that help decision-makers determine cost-effectiveness, cost-efficiency, and cost benefits. This objective carries the weight of two competencies (as was the case with Interim Objective Number Six). You are expected to be creative and to perform at the synthesis level. Only one recycle will be permitted for completion of this objective and students failing to achieve the objective on the first try will be given an "I" in the course until they have had one recycle opportunity.

Author Index

Subject Index